WHY
SOCIALISM
STRUGGLES

Dr. DOUG CARDELL

WHY

SOCIALISM

STRUGGLES

[EXPOSING THE ECONOMIC ERRORS
THAT UNDERMINE UTOPIAN IDEALS]

GREENLEAF
BOOK GROUP PRESS

Published by Greenleaf Book Group Press
Austin, Texas
www.gbgpress.com

Distributed by Greenleaf Book Group

For ordering information or special discounts for bulk purchases, please contact
Greenleaf Book Group at PO Box 91869, Austin, TX 78709, 512.891.6100.

Design and composition by Greenleaf Book Group
Cover design by Greenleaf Book Group

Publisher's Cataloging-in-Publication data is available.

Print ISBN: 979-8-88645-444-4

eBook ISBN: 979-8-88645-445-1

To offset the number of trees consumed in the printing of our books, Greenleaf
donates a portion of the proceeds from each printing to the Arbor Day
Foundation. Greenleaf Book Group has replaced over 50,000 trees since 2007.

Printed in the United States of America on acid-free paper

26 27 28 29 30 31   10 9 8 7 6 5 4 3 2 1

First Edition

Contents

Introduction

Why *Socialism Struggles* is a book of questions and answers. Taken as a whole, it is the answer to the question "Why does socialism struggle?" Each chapter answers a main question, followed by smaller questions and answers related to the main topic in each chapter. This question and answer (Q&A) approach mirrors my time as an economist and college professor, where I have spent most of my professional time answering questions like the ones in this book.

If you're reading this book, chances are you are either for or against socialism or think you are. I say, "or think you are" because even the most well-informed folks I talk to don't really understand what socialism and its alternatives are. My intent in this book is to clearly explain what socialism is and to unravel the lies you have probably been told about socialism. As an economist I have received countless questions over the years about socialism and other economies. The questions often arise because many people today confuse true socialism—economic dictatorship—with the social democracies of Canada and Europe.

Social democracies and true socialism are at opposite ends of the economic spectrum. I wrote this book in part as a warning to those who are confusing the two, in hopes that you will understand the distinction before our own democracy here in the United States unwittingly becomes a socialist dictatorship. This is not something I want, and I'm willing to bet most of you, once you understand what true socialism is, do not want that either.

I titled this book *Why Socialism Struggles* for one very simple reason: Socialism doesn't work. However, most people don't know why. In the pages ahead, I show you, in a conversational Q&A format, why socialism is bad for any economy.

WHY THIS BOOK?

I wrote this book in a simple, easy-to-understand format to make these economic principles more accessible to others. Each chapter is filled with questions that I have been asked many times, questions that you may also have wanted to ask, along with my responses to the questions. Hopefully, you will soon discover that this book is not just any economics book. The way I take complex topics and make them more accessible for those who aren't economic students or theorists is unique and by design. Economics affects each of us. Every decision anyone has ever made or ever will make is an economic decision. Most people think economics is about money, but it's so much more than that. Economics is the study of how we make the best use of what we have. We have limited resources and a wide variety of choices we can use them for. It's true that money is a limited resource, but so are things like time, material assets, muscular endurance, patience, and reputation.

Every decision you make is basically deciding what resources you are going to trade. For example, right now you are choosing to use a limited resource, your time, to read this book. You have thousands of other ways you could spend your time right now. For example, you could take a walk, watch television, or hang out with friends. Whether you realize it or not, your choice is an economic decision even though no money, goods, or services are involved.

According to a widely circulated estimate, the average adult makes thirty-five thousand decisions a day. Every one of those decisions is an economic choice, including your decision to read this book. I wrote this book to help you understand how the world works so you can take more conscious control of your own decision-making. The more you understand about real-world economics, the more likely you are to reject socialism.

This book is about socialism, and as you find out the truth about economics (and that most of what you've been taught is wrong), you'll find that socialism and its cousins—fascism and communism—are not workable economic systems. They are built on a narrow ideology that ignores basic economic principles and instead wishes for a substitute reality that does not and cannot ever exist in the actual human world. Socialism in its true form threatens the health of any thriving economy and restricts your ability to make the most basic of decisions, from what to eat for dinner to what to watch on TV.

In fact, every country that has experimented with socialism, or any form of central economic planning for that matter, has suffered from it. Most countries abandoned the attempt, and the few that didn't eventually destroyed their national economies.

AN ECONOMIC CROSSROADS

The United States is at an economic crossroads. Public pressure from "progressive" activists and politicians has been somewhat successful in convincing some members of the public to move the United States government toward socialism, which increasingly influences public policy. While many of these proposals are closer to fascism than socialism, the difference is hardly significant, given that both systems require the government to plan and control the economy and diminish or eliminate free-market capitalism.

As I see it, the US economy has three choices: turning left, turning right, or going straight ahead. The road left leads toward a centrally planned economy, which is either socialism, fascism, or communism. The road right leads to a smaller federal government and less government control of the economy. The road straight ahead continues the current mix of policies that divides us and seems to satisfy no one.

The disagreement about economic policy is one factor that is dividing this country. Polling data released by the Gallup organization in 2017 comparing 2000–2001 and 2016–2017 shows a 44 percent increase in divisiveness regarding the size of the federal government in the past fourteen years. The data also indicates that divisiveness on the degree to which the government should be responsible for health care has increased 23 percent in fifteen years. Finally, it shows that the belief that "upper income" people pay too little taxes has increased in its divisiveness by 13 percent in fourteen years.[1] Those are all economic issues that are increasingly dividing our country. Answering which path leads to greater economic good may mitigate or reverse this increasing and harmful divisiveness.

Divisiveness is just a symptom. Even if divisiveness were not an issue, we are at a crossroads. Without complete and accurate information about which path is most likely to lead to the desired outcome, policymakers and the public risk disastrous results. The question is whether socialism can produce a more significant benefit for the population than free-market capitalism. To understand why socialism doesn't work, we need to learn what economics is and how it functions.

No government has ever succeeded in running a centrally planned economy for more than a few years. Whether it would be more fair or not—if it ever succeeded—is debatable, but it cannot succeed. One of the requirements for effective government planning of the economy is its ability to make accurate economic forecasts, and that is not possible. Many systems, capitalism for example, don't rely on forecasts since the government does not plan the economy. However, under socialism the government must depend on forecasts, since it assumes control of all economic planning.

While many economic predictions exist, most are no more reliable than flipping a coin, and they are too inaccurate to support a planned economy. It's not up to me to say if you or anyone is right or wrong based on the economic system you support. What I can do is show you how socialist ideas play out in the real world and the economic consequences of them. Once you've seen these ideas and understand their consequences, I think your perspective is likely to change, but either way, I'm not here to judge your beliefs or to get you to think differently. While I am an economist and have spent years investigating economics and learning about the world economy and how it works (or doesn't work), if the concepts in this book don't ring true for you, don't believe them just because I say so. All I ask is that you read with an open mind and use your own discernment as you continue.

THE THREAT OF SOCIALISM

As I said earlier, our country is at an economic crossroads where the threat of socialism has never been stronger. When I enlisted in the military, I took an oath to defend the United States against all enemies, foreign and domestic. That oath didn't come with an expiration date. And for that reason, it is my duty to warn you of this current (and very real) threat to our democracy. The growing belief that socialism can solve our problems better than free-market capitalism will be our undoing unless we choose the right path.

Some of you may be wondering how socialism can even be a threat. Maybe you even lean in that direction now and are starting to think free-market capitalism is the problem. If you feel this way, you are not alone. Many Americans are starting to question the capitalist society in which we live. While the focus of this book is on socialism, in which the government takes ownership of the means of production, I want to give you some context by sharing what economics is really about, outlining what economic systems exist, and explaining why some succeed and others fail.

In a free market like ours in the United States, we are given the opportunity to prosper to the greatest extent possible. Along with the opportunity to succeed comes the opportunity to fail. Many of socialism's problems are due to the efforts to prevent those failures. But every economic endeavor is an experiment, and only by these experiments can we find the most productive route. Failures are not a problem; they are part of the solution, and free-market capitalism is the only system proven to use these successes and failures to create the greatest possible economic good for its citizens.

FREE-MARKET CAPITALISM

As you will find as you read on, true free-market capitalism has only existed for brief periods before being manipulated by governments. Most of the "problems" associated with free-market capitalism are the result of these manipulations. Of course, it is important to challenge what isn't working, but it is equally important to do your homework and learn why capitalism isn't working and to research the surest methods of improving it. In free-market capitalism you have the right to vote. You have the right to own property. Your rights to life, liberty, and pursuit of property are protected. You can go to the store and buy anything you can afford. However, under socialism, as you will learn in the chapters ahead, none of these rights and freedoms exist.

The word *capitalism* is often misused and misunderstood. In fact, the misuse of the terms *free market* and *capitalism* suffer from many of the same misunderstandings as socialism does. Free-market capitalism helps all of us. The wealthy are not the only ones who benefit in this type of economy. Free-market capitalism has lifted more people out of poverty than any other system—far more than most realize. Of course, the system can be improved, and we'll discuss that in detail as well.

Within free-market capitalism, both individuals and corporations get to own capital goods. We get to choose what to invest in, what to eat, what to buy, and so on. These decisions aren't made for us like they are in a socialist society. I explain within these pages how some economic systems work better than others. And some don't work at all. In the first chapter, we define the various economic systems and create the framework necessary to discuss economics in a meaningful way.

I hope you will enjoy reading this book and that you will gain insights that will help you improve your life as well as the life of your community, your region, and your country.

[1]

What Is Socialism?

What is socialism?

True socialism is an economic system in which the government owns all real property and the means of production. In true socialism there are no private companies, no private farms, no private living spaces, and no freedom to buy or sell. All commerce is controlled by the government. Some countries that fall into this category are North Korea, Venezuela, and Cuba. In these countries, the government has complete control of the economy.

But I thought Cuba was a communist country. Why are you including it under socialism?

To place socialism in its true context, we need to examine all the alternate economic systems. In Figure 1, you will notice that Cuba falls under the category of true socialism and is an economic dictatorship, not communist, which I will explain further in a minute. As you can see, it is one of the countries at the extreme

Economic anarchy	Economic freedom				Economic dictatorship
	Degree of economic freedom				
Failed states	**Free**	**Mostly free**	**Moderately free**	**Mostly unfree**	**Fascist/socialist**
These states have too little government to protect property and commerce, which restricts innovation and motivation and inhibits economic growth.	These states have just enough government control to guarantee real and intellectual property rights, encouraging innovation and motivation and stimulating economic growth.	These states are doing well but would do better with more freedom. They have adequate protections but have restrictions and limitations that hamper economic growth.	These states would benefit from a good deal more freedom. They have restrictions and limitations that reduce innovation and motivation and limit economic growth.	These states are so repressed that growth is limited. They have so little freedom that innovation and motivation are minimized, severely limiting economic growth.	These states have absolute government control of the economy, which restricts innovation and motivation and inhibits or prevents economic growth.
Examples: Libya Somalia Syria Yemen	**Examples:** Singapore Switzerland Ireland Taiwan	**Examples:** New Zealand Nordic countries South Korea United States	**Examples:** United Kingdom Japan France Mexico	**Examples:** Nicaragua Russia India Rwanda	**Examples:** China Venezuela Cuba North Korea

Figure 1. Economic systems

end of the economic spectrum, along with North Korea, China, and Venezuela.

To the far left in Figure 1 (not to be confused with political ideology), you will see the other extreme, including Yemen, Libya, Somalia, and Syria. These are what economists term *failed states*. That is, they are countries in name only. Yemen, for example, is a mishmash of as many as four hundred Zaydi tribes—that mostly adhere to the Zaydi branch of Shia Islam—in the north and hereditary castes in the urban areas. This lack of unifying forces has led to almost constant friction and civil war. A government in this kind of disarray cannot provide the necessary safeguards that allow an economy to function. This includes protection of property rights, protection from crime, a functioning monetary system, and more. In failed states, the government does not provide sufficient protection for private property to allow the economy to function. And who would want to start a store or a factory in a country where your goods are not safe from thieves and bandits? These failed states are the opposite extreme from socialism.

Okay, I see what you're saying about Yemen, but you said these were not socialist countries.

That's true. Socialism means complete control of the economy by the government, and failed states have little or no control of the economy—not enough control to function. If we compare Yemen to a country on the opposite end of the economic spectrum, North Korea, the difference is clearer. In North Korea the government has total control of the economy and everything else. It has a socialist dictatorship. In a socialist dictatorship, no one can pursue their legitimate self-interest because the state determines the interests and values that will be followed.

Yemen and North Korea, while opposites economically, are two of the poorest countries in the world. While neither country provides exact data, most economists, including myself, estimate their total economic output (per capita GDP) between $500 and $1,500 per person per year. This extreme poverty happens because no control (Yemen) and absolute control (North Korea) both prevent economic growth. Neither end of the spectrum honors the values and choices of the citizens. This is why both ends of the economic spectrum must fail. They are not sustainable economic systems. For an economy to survive—and there are many that do—the government must have enough power to protect its citizens but not so much that it can interfere with their economic choices.

How many economic systems are there, and how are they different?

No two countries have the same system, and most of the names folks call systems are incorrect or confusing. If you take another look at Figure 1, you can get a sense of how diverse economic systems are.

Why aren't communism and democratic socialism on the chart?

They are not on the chart because communism and democratic socialism are both myths. Neither has ever existed. Communism is an imagined state in which socialism has become so successful that government is no longer necessary, but socialism has never become successful, so this has never happened.

Democratic socialism is also imaginary. By that I mean it is imaginary in the sense that it has never existed as the economy of a nation. Those who call themselves democratic socialists see it as a road to true socialism. The website of the Democratic Socialists of America says: "We must replace it [capitalism] with democratic socialism, a system where ordinary people have a real voice in our workplaces, neighborhoods, and society. We believe there are many avenues that feed into the democratic road to socialism."[1] What the democratic socialists wish for is an imaginary economy, which has never been implemented because democracy and socialism are inherently incompatible. Can they achieve true socialism? It's too early to tell. However, the Democratic Socialist Party says democratic socialism is a waypoint leading to genuine socialism.

But what about Europe? They have socialist countries, and they work.

Many people cite the social democracies of Europe as examples of democratic socialism, but they are not. They are capitalist countries that have a larger social safety net than the United States. These governments have not taken over all property and the means of production in the economies of any of these countries. The Nordic countries, Great Britain, and Canada call themselves social democracies. They all enjoy free-market capitalism as their basic economic structure but have a more extensive public welfare system than some other countries.

Some of them have socialized medicine; that is, the government has nationalized or taken ownership of the health-care system. Some have nationalized the education system. Is this sustainable, or will they eventually have to choose between free markets and true socialism? It's too early to tell. Experiments like this take decades to play out.

But it is important to understand that the social democracies of Europe are not socialist countries; nor are they planned economies. Welfare-state capitalism is the best way to characterize them. They use the term *social democracy* to mean a democracy that is socially conscious. While the words *social* and *socialist* sound similar, they refer to completely different ideas. In many ways, some social democracies have economies that are less restricted and controlled than the US economy, as we see in Figure 1. Democratic socialism is an oxymoron. Democracy and socialism are incompatible.

So, now that we have dealt with the myth of socialism in the Nordic countries and others, we are ready to address the original question: Can socialism be the economic system of a democratic country? Of course, a democratic government can and has elected socialists, and some have established socialist governments. After World War II, the United Kingdom, India, and Israel all adopted socialism. In all three countries, the system was initially successful but failed after a decade or two, when those planning their economies proved unable to react quickly enough to changing economic conditions. All three then returned to some form of free-market capitalism, though they retained relatively large welfare states.

> **Democratic socialism is an oxymoron.**
> **Democracy and socialism are incompatible.**

Unfortunately, some elected socialists have quickly taken all power, and the countries have become dictatorships. The ones that did not become dictatorships did not because the persons in power were voted out, and their economies returned to free markets. Will the social democracies' systems eventually lead to true socialism? That doesn't seem likely. In fact, the trend in most of those countries is to retreat toward less government instead of more.

I was taught that fascism and socialism are opposites. Why do you have them together?

It's interesting that some teach that fascism and socialism are opposites, given that the best-known example of fascism is Nazi Germany. The word *Nazi* is a contraction for National Socialist German Workers' Party, often called the National Socialists. Fascism and socialism are both based on centrally planned economies. In fascism, the government directly *controls* the means of production, and in socialism, the government *owns* the means of production, but in both cases, the government has total control of the economy. Does it make sense to label two forms of absolute economic control as opposites? No. I say this because the opposite of absolute control is no control or economic chaos, as in the failed states such as Yemen. The differences that have existed between some fascist countries and some socialist countries are not economic. For example, Nazi Germany was fascist but also nationalist and rejected Marx's notion of class conflict, while socialist Russia sought world government under communism. These differences are not economic but ideological.

While there is considerable confusion about what socialism, fascism, and free-market capitalism are and, possibly more importantly, what they are not, some definitions and explanations are warranted. Communism, socialism, and fascism are examples of centrally planned economies (CPEs). *Merriam-Webster* defines a CPE as an economic system in which the elements of an economy (such as labor, capital, and natural resources) are subject to government control and regulation designed to achieve the objectives of a comprehensive economic development plan.

Lately, the words *socialism* and *fascism* have been carelessly bandied about in ways that muddy and confuse the issue. For example, the preceding definition clarifies what a CPE is, but many use socialism to refer to other concepts such as an expanded welfare state, fascist economic controls, or a vague picture of a "friendlier" government.

Recent proposals to forgive student loans, while economically unsound, are not socialist, but an expansion of the welfare state. Those calling for Medicare for all or wage and price controls are not advocating a socialist takeover of the economy but fascist economic control. And those who think socialist refers to a friendlier government, thinking that socialist is nice, like social media or an ice cream social, don't know that socialism is actually antisocial. Just ask anyone from a true socialist country.

Can you say more about capitalism?

Merriam-Webster defines *capitalism* as an economic system characterized by private or corporate ownership of capital goods, by investments that are determined by private decisions, and by prices, production, and the distribution of goods that are determined mainly by competition in a free market. As discussed earlier, the definition of socialism includes the government ownership of all property; investments determined solely by the government; and prices, production, and distribution all under government control. In free-market capitalism, everything is owned by the people. Whereas in socialism, everything is owned by the government.

The misuse of the terms *free market* and *capitalism* creates many of the same misunderstandings as socialism. The word *capitalism* is the most misused and misunderstood. To understand many of the misunderstandings about socialism and capitalism, we will need to learn more about economics in general.

Capitalism relies on spontaneous order rather than government control to keep the economy in balance. Spontaneous order may seem like a contradiction in terms, but it is a common natural process. Spontaneous order is a state in which a collection of independent entities operating in their best interests create an organized system without any central control. There are many examples of spontaneous order in both nature and societies. Herd animals, the human body, and the free market are some examples.

You may have read about how a flock of birds changes direction without a leader. The flock can do this because each individual bird reacts only to the birds next to it. Many researchers have used that as an example of spontaneous order. They believe, and their mathematical models support the idea, that birds and many other animals try to keep a minimum distance between themselves and others so that if one moves, they all move.

Spontaneous order in the animal kingdom is evident in virtually all herding animals. The scientific interest in why animals, particularly prey animals, organize in herds has been a research subject in biology, physics, and psychology for quite some time. Scientists have postulated that herding behavior might result from individual herd members' self-interested motivation to reduce their own predation risk, even at the expense of other herd members. Their intentions are not to hurt others but to protect themselves. For example, the herd members might be competing for the safest places within the herd.

Recently, scientists have created computer models that seem to verify this hypothesis. These simulations indicate that herd members trying to reduce individual vulnerability tend to form tight-knit groups. This grouping behavior exists in a variety of species. Furthermore, these models demonstrate that the individual motivation to minimize predation risk leads to group actions, including constant movement within the herd. This continuous motion results in an equal sharing of predation risk among herd members, each acting in their best interests.

The herd exists only to help its members. I say this because as herds form, the average risk decreases until they achieve the minimum individual risk. After that, the average risk varies slightly, while individual member risk at any particular time varies dramatically. However, the average individual risk remains constant. Therefore, it is in everyone's self-interest to keep the group functioning.

For example, imagine a herd of fifty or so animals. Because of terrain, wind direction, or lighting conditions, the herd is concerned about threats from the south, so members on the south side of the herd move within the pack to the north. Now the center, the safest place in the pack, has shifted to the north and exposes new members on the south side to greater risk, so they begin to move to the north, which moves the center again and exposes a new group of members. Because of these actions, every herd member spends the same amount of time in every position, equalizing their risks across the herd. Of course, each member is pursuing their self-interest. Still, the result is equally shared risk without a leader to direct the action. In other words, the order is spontaneously generated. When each member of the herd pursues their self-interest and assumes the other members are pursuing theirs, the result is equality.

How does this relate to us?

Spontaneous order is similar to how the human body or any complex organism functions. The conscious mind cannot regulate the mechanisms that allow a body, a complex living organism, to flourish. Instead, organisms' cells act in their best interest and do what they must to live, grow, and reproduce. Occasionally, the process goes wrong, as in cancer, when corrupted cells pursuing their best interests produce an undesirable result for the organism. Conscious effort, in the form of treatment, is required to control rogue cells pursuing their own best interests. This is analogous to government intervention in a crime wave. Cancer is to the body what a failing state is to the economy. However, too much conscious control is equally problematic.

Imagine the extra brainpower that would be required to

directly manage the twenty to forty trillion cells in the human body. Consciously directing one cell every second would take hundreds of thousands of years to give every cell a command. In addition, the human body contains more foreign microbial cells than human body cells. Obviously, these foreign cells are beyond the control of the conscious mind. None of these alien or human cells are aware of the body as an organism. From the cells' point of view, the body is simply the environment in which they reside. From their vantage point, the human body is like any other complex ecosystem—it functions smoothly, without direction, with every system member acting in their best interests and adapting to changes and stresses imposed by other members.

Are all ecosystems examples of spontaneous order?

Yes. While squirrels are fundamental in planting new trees and bees are essential in pollinating plants, neither squirrels nor bees think of these actions as their jobs. To squirrels and bees, nuts and pollen are just food.

In the context of economics, spontaneous order refers to the idea that the economy is a self-organizing system in which the actions of individuals and firms interacting in markets lead to the efficient allocation of resources and the spontaneous emergence of complex economic structures, such as prices, firms, and industries. The economy is just another ecosystem.

As in the previous examples, economic systems work best when every system member pursues their self-interest. This pursuit is similar to the foregoing examples of cells and squirrels and bees. For example, the cells in your liver could not do their job as well if they had to think about how their actions affected brain cells or bone cells. Instead, these cells must devote themselves to doing what they do best—keeping your liver functioning. The squirrels in the forest have their hands full being squirrels, and they have neither the capacity nor the information to contemplate how their actions affect other wildlife. Similarly, bees do not consider how their actions affect birds and butterflies; they are too busy being bees.

But isn't self-interest selfish?

Self-interest and selfishness are not the same thing. When children play, self-interest might exhibit itself by one child taking a toy from another so they can have a turn playing with it. Whereas selfish behavior might be taking a toy from another solely to deprive the other. In the forest, squirrels gathering nuts is self-interest, but it would be selfish if squirrels gathered flowers they could not eat just to deprive the bees.

The undirected drive of what some think of as subordinate entities—such as cells in the body or producers and consumers in an economy—to pursue their best interests is natural and ultimately beneficial. It explains why there is always a flourishing black market in countries that have tried central economic planning. These black markets are the ultimate proof that central planning is not what the citizens of a nation want or need. Producers and consumers want to be free to negotiate value and pursue their best interests and individual life choices in the manner that only free-market capitalism provides.

With spontaneous order, do we really need government regulation?

We need government regulation to protect the people and the economy. Like the human body sometimes suffers from cancer, a corruption of cellular self-interest, the economic body sometimes suffers from similar corruption. In cancer, the brain must take control and seek treatment. That is similar to a legitimate role of government in preventing similar corruption in the economy. But preventing corruption is not the same as controlling the economy. Spontaneous order preserves the natural order of the economy. The free market is impressive because it can order an economy without direction. It is as legitimate and normal as anything in nature. The spontaneous order created by the combination of individual choices that make up the free market can order an economy in the best interests of the citizenry. No other economic system has ever provided greater good to more people.

That sounds a lot like anarchy. How can that be good?

Spontaneous order is not anarchy. On the contrary, it is a natural order that arises from individual interactions without a central planner. Furthermore, comparing CPEs with spontaneously generated free markets has consistently produced the same results:

Free markets always produce greater economic benefits and higher living standards than planned economies. The evidence shows that a CPE cannot result in greater economic good than can be achieved by spontaneous order, as is created by the combination of individual choices that make up the free market.

Socialism is a form of economic dictatorship, and the only viable alternative is free-market capitalism. Every country experimenting with socialism or any form of central economic planning has suffered from it. Most abandoned the attempt, and the few that didn't eventually destroyed their national economies. In free-market capitalism the economy is in the hands of the people. I think as we learn more about economics you'll see why I'm concerned even if you don't agree with my position on socialism.

SUMMARY: What Is Socialism?

As we learned in this chapter, economic systems with too little or too much control will eventually fail. Spontaneous order is a natural organizing system that drives free-market capitalism. In capitalism, the values of the people drive the economy. The people vote on what gets made and sold by choosing what to buy. While some government intervention is needed for spontaneous order to work well, the people's choices overrule the government's choices.

Socialism and fascism are CPEs. It is impossible to centrally plan an economy and leave the people free in other respects. That is why socialism always leads to dictatorship. Without the ability to make economic choices—to choose what you own, where you live, and what job you have—what does freedom mean?

Democratic socialism and communism do not exist. The social democracies of Europe are not democratic socialist countries. Democratic socialism would be a state in which the economy was under the control of the state with a government that is popularly elected. It's never happened for more than very brief periods. Communism has never happened because it is a highly evolved form of socialism, and socialism has never succeeded long enough to get there.

Socialism and fascism are not opposites as many have been taught. Though the two have minor technical differences, they are both CPEs. Calling them opposites is like calling giant sequoia and giant redwoods opposite because they have differences such as shape and hardiness. They are both really big trees, and the opposite would be a really small tree, maybe a dwarf willow that rarely gets as tall as three inches.

Spontaneous order is an amazing natural process that allows a system to order itself without direction. Your body is an excellent example, as most of your body's functioning is beyond your control. The vast majority is even beyond your awareness, yet your body functions spontaneously without you having to direct it. Spontaneous order occasionally benefits from intervention. In the body, illness is a good example. People live longer today than a hundred years ago because medical interventions have improved.

> **Economic systems work best when every system member pursues their self-interest. There is a big difference between self-interest and selfishness.**

Economic systems work best when every system member pursues their self-interest. There is a big difference between self-interest and selfishness. Self-interest is necessary for any organism, including you, to survive. Selfishness goes beyond survival and is usually against one's self-interest. Selfishness is taking from others by stealth or force to get more for yourself or simply to deprive others.

[2]

What Is Economics?

What is economics anyway? Isn't it just about money?

Economics includes money, but there's more to it than that. Economics is the study of how we choose to allocate our resources. Every living thing must make economic decisions to survive. If an organism burns more calories looking for food than it gains in calories from the food it finds, it dies. Economics is the study of how to make choices about the best use of finite resources that can be used in more than one way. True, money is that kind of a finite resource but so are material assets, time, strength, and patience.

Every decision is the evaluation of a trade of one thing for another. A choice between going for a hike and taking a nap is an economic decision, even though no money or products are involved. Going for a hike may improve your health or sense of well-being, but taking a nap may provide some needed rest. Either way, a finite resource will be used up—time. There is more than one use for this finite resource, so your choice is an economic decision. Economics studies how people make choices, although it applies to all living things—even plants.

You mean plants can make choices?

Choice does not necessarily mean conscious choice. If you put a plant in a room with a window, it must "decide" which way to grow, and it will grow toward the window where the light is better. However, I don't think the plant *thinks* to make that decision. It might be instinct; it might be innate programming. I really don't know how plants make the choices they make, but they obviously do.

Plants and other living things don't behave randomly. Their behavior is usually predictable. Nonliving things don't make choices; how they react is random. If you flip a coin, you can't predict the outcome. Nonliving things may sometimes seem to behave consistently, but that is a result of humans making choices and constructing nonliving things to execute them.

An electrician can install a light switch that turns on a light predictably, but that results from human action. Engineers can design computers that can perform almost human-like tasks. But even the most advanced artificial intelligence is artificial—a result of human programming. However, if you put a plant in a room with a window, it will grow toward the light without an engineer programming it to do so.

Economics is the study of choices. Every living thing makes economic decisions. Let's say you've got a cow and some hay, and you put bales of hay one hundred feet away and five hundred feet away. Where will the cow go? To the closest one, of course, but why? At some level, the cow *knows* that food is calories and moving requires calories, so the cow will choose the option that provides the most calories while expending the fewest calories to get there. Now, just like with plants, I don't know how this happens. I don't think cows can make calorie calculations, but I know they behave as if they do.

So, when you're training a dog, you're using economics?

Exactly. When you train a dog, you present choices. For example, if you say "sit" and the dog sits, he gets something he wants, like a treat or extra attention. If the dog doesn't sit, he doesn't get a treat. The dog learns that if he chooses to sit when you say "sit," he gets a reward. All living things seem to choose to do those things they have learned will benefit them and avoid doing things that might cause them harm.

All organisms seek to improve their condition. I'd go so far as to say every choice is an economic decision. In other words, every decision any organism makes requires giving up something to get something else. For example, a cow must give up calories by burning them while walking to the food, but when it gets there, it will get more calories to replace them and more besides. The dog gives up getting to do what he was doing before you said "sit" and, in return, gets the treat. All action is purposeful; the action happens only in response to a purpose. Animals may appear to us sometimes to be wandering around aimlessly, but they seem to sense that the more they know about their environment, the better off they will be. So they explore. Organisms act only when they have a reason. This is true even if the organism is incapable of understanding the reason for its action.

But when a bee stings you, it dies. How does that help the bee?

When a bee stings and, therefore, dies, it is not acting against its own interest. Most of the evidence indicates that bees don't *know* that stinging will result in death. Unlike humans, who can watch YouTube videos or read books about others' experiences and learn from them, lower organisms can only learn from experience. Bees don't get a chance to come back to life to learn from the experience. However, even if the bee did *know* it would die, it may somehow *know* that it's more important to protect the hive. It responds to the threat the only way it knows how. All action is an attempt to create a better state than the current one. No organism knowingly chooses to make things worse for itself.

But people go to war. They run into burning buildings to save others. Isn't that choosing to make things worse for themselves?

Great question! That brings us to a key economic concept—the idea of value. People are far more complex than other animals. We can place value on nonmaterial things.

You mentioned war; soldiers are trained to value duty, honor, and country. They are trained to protect and defend their brothers and sisters in arms. Nathan Hale was a twenty-one-year-old American patriot and a soldier in the American Revolution. Hale valued duty and honor above life. He was assigned spy missions in New York at great risk to himself. He was eventually caught and executed. A British captain, John Montresor, reported that his last words were, "I only regret that I have but one life to lose for my country."[1]

Like Nathan Hale, we all have within us an ordered list of values—what we value most, second most, third most, and so on. We are always willing to trade something lower on the list for something higher. What makes understanding others so difficult is these lists are different for every person. They are as unique as DNA or fingerprints. No two people have the same list, and even the same person regularly changes their list. Their list may include conditions and even appear a bit "jumbly" at times, and sometimes, a person's values may conflict with one another. Sometimes, this list is overridden by emotional impulses, but this list affects all of our decisions.

So, are you saying our choices come from our values?

Yes. Furthermore, those choices lead to actions and behaviors. I'd like to introduce you to the ABCs of economics—action, behavior, and choice. Actions are the result of choices. This seems to be true of all life—cows, plants, and people. Behavior is a pattern of consistent actions that stem from consistent choices. You could think of behaviors as automatic choices. After making similar choices repeatedly, the organism no longer consciously chooses. It simply responds by habit or instinct. For example, if I toss a ball toward you, you won't stop and think, am I going to catch this ball or not? You just do it. You made the choice a long time ago that when things are thrown to you, you'll catch them. It has become an automatic choice. It has become a behavior. Actions lead to behaviors and are determined by choices: ABC.

But people often make poor choices. Shouldn't we make them do what is best for themselves?

All organisms learn by experimentation. They try something and observe the consequences. These experiments are choices, and the organism learns from the results of those choices. Some people seem to be really good at observing others' choices and results and using those results to allow them to learn without performing their own experiments. Some read books and watch YouTube videos. Others are less prone to learn from others and instead conduct their own experiments. When these experiments produce undesirable results, we call them mistakes. But the result of an experiment is not a mistake; it's a way to learn.

If someone else makes choices for others, three negative effects can occur. First, there's the value problem. Making a choice for someone assumes that the chooser and the choosee share the same values, but that is never true; no two people have the same values. Second, making choices for someone else deprives them of the chance to learn. If you see a child about to put their hand on a hot stove, you should stop them. But then have them lick their finger and tap it briefly. The child is not harmed but learns about hot stoves. Limiting the damage caused by an experiment is fine, but having enough of a consequence to allow for learning is best. Third, making choices for someone else deprives them of a fundamental aspect of their humanity: freedom of choice. All organisms make choices, and without the ability to do that, they are functionally dead.

What about someone who insists on destructive behavior like alcoholism? Shouldn't someone intervene in cases like these?

Most experts on alcoholism will tell you that if the drinker doesn't want to stop drinking, they won't. Short of keeping them locked up and away from alcohol, they will continue to drink. All you can do is keep offering help and letting them know that you'll be there when they're ready. I don't know why an alcoholic would choose to refuse treatment, but I have to believe that, at some level, they feel sobriety would be worse. That wouldn't be my choice, but everyone has a different value list, so I'm not in a position to judge their choice.

But does an addict really have a choice?

They have a choice of wanting to stop and seeking treatment or not. They may not be able to stop without help, but before they can get help, they must choose to try. All action by any organism is an attempt to transform the current situation into a state that more closely resembles their values—that is, to improve their existence, however they define that. They do this by making choices and acting on them.

Why is choice necessary?

Since the future is unknown, choice is necessary. And this choice is what motivates action. If the future were known, there would be no need for choice and no need for action, and all life would cease. If you see a tornado coming, you quickly make choices. Do you get in a shelter, try to outrun it, or stay put and hope your house stays intact? You have to choose because you don't know what will happen. But if the future is known, if you *know*, for sure, that the tornado is going to destroy your house and kill you, there is no choice to make. Knowing the future means that there is a certain, unchangeable future. If the future were certain and unchangeable, no action by any organism would have a purpose. Why do anything if nothing matters? The fact that the future is unknowable makes choice necessary. When you see the tornado coming, you must make a choice because you don't know what will happen, and that creates alternative possible futures that you are able to choose between.

For example, choosing to buy health insurance is a choice that results in the action of paying premiums and getting regular medical checkups. If you know the future, then that future is fixed. If you knew you were going to live another forty years, *no matter what*, and nothing could change that, then why look both ways when crossing the street or buy health insurance? You are going to live another forty years regardless. This fixed future would happen no matter what you did, so taking action is unnecessary. Choice is necessary for action. Without choice, action stops, and without action, life stops. Since economics is the study of choice, it is also the study of the foundation of life. Learning to make the best choices leads to the best life.

Furthermore, successful action as a result of choices produces a desired result—some product of the action taken. The action changes the world. Of course, unsuccessful action also produces a result and changes the world. Many successful actions produce unintended consequences that are less desirable, and many unsuccessful actions produce beneficial consequences. These actions transform and rearrange what exists. True creation begins in the mind. Acting on that mental creation results in a transformation, a change, in the physical world.

I have many examples of this in my life, and if you think about it, I'm sure you will recognize many in your own. For example, on my way to a final exam in college, I chose to take an alternate route, a shortcut on a dirt road that I thought would get me there faster. The road was poorly maintained, and I got a flat tire that made me miss the first half of the exam. I went through the exam as fast as I could and finished just as time ran out. Only I and another student were left. She was really smart but a very careful test taker. As we were the only ones left, I invited her to lunch, and she has been my wife now for almost fifty years. My unsuccessful action—taking a shortcut that ended up taking longer than my usual route—resulted in a wonderfully beneficial but unintended consequence.

But wouldn't many changes have a negative effect on society?

Some changes have a negative effect on some members of society. That's true. Society is nothing more than people acting together, cooperating to produce a mutually beneficial result. Like the members of the herd we discussed earlier, shifting positions within the herd exposes some members to greater risk, but the average risk is lower. In the long run, every member of the herd is better off.

People cooperating leads to specialization as individuals exercise their unique gifts and abilities and trade with others to satisfy their needs and wants. This division of labor is far more productive for everyone in the group and may be the most defining factor separating us from animals. However, the development of specialization disadvantaged the folks who wanted to be completely independent. The best thing you can do to benefit society is to legitimately pursue your own self-interest. If everyone does what they can to improve their well-being without harming others, both the individuals and the society benefit.

Isn't that just selfishness? Shouldn't we do what's best for society?

No. Most of us have a strong value in helping others. So, when you are helping others, you are doing something rewarding for yourself. This makes you feel good. When we help others, we are pursuing our self-interest in helping others. Legitimate self-interest is the pursuit of our values. This means we are always looking to trade something we value less for something we value more. For example, if I supply a person who is homeless with a temporary place to stay while they seek something permanent, I am trading my value of the space provided and the inconvenience it causes me for the higher value of helping someone in need.

> ## When individuals suppress their self-interest for "the good of the group," the group and all the individuals in it suffer.

When individuals suppress their self-interest for "the good of the group," the group and all the individuals in it suffer. This seems completely counterintuitive, but it is true and explainable. Since no one can reliably know what is best for another, how can we hope to know what is best for an entire group? If we try, we will dilute the effort of the group. Since the total output benefits the group, lowering the total output hurts everyone in the group. This is precisely what has happened every time the well-being of the group has been valued more than the well-being of the individual. And can a society of unfulfilled individuals be rightly called a success? Placing the needs of the group above the needs of its members cannot succeed because instead of harnessing human nature for the good of all, it relies on everyone working hard against their own self-interest.

Imagine what would happen if squirrels and bees tried to help each other. Since squirrels can't fly and bees can't carry acorns, both groups would become less effective. Some would die, fewer trees would be planted, and fewer plants would be pollinated. Eventually, the entire environment would suffer. The group is successful when bees do their bee thing, and when squirrels just be the best squirrels they can be.

In another example, I had an auto mechanic fifty years ago who had a sign in his shop: "Labor is $10 an hour. If you watch, it's $15 an hour. If you help, it's $25 an hour." He understood that he could do his best work for the customer if he were free to focus on doing his best.

I wrote this book as an economist, and one of my talents is the ability to explain complicated concepts in a way that noneconomists understand. However, I am the world's worst proofreader. I reread something and see what was meant rather than what was said. My editor sees what I actually wrote and has a superior knowledge of English grammar. For example, my editor noted that I used the word *things* 120 times and replaced the word *thing* with the word it referred to. I would never have noticed that because I knew what thing I meant, but the reader likely would not. If we lived in a socialist country, our jobs would be assigned to us based primarily on what the government thought was needed at the moment. So we could find ourselves reversing roles. My wonderful editor, with a degree in English, might be forced to write the economics book, and an economist with no talent for editing might have to edit that book. The entire society would be made worse off because the book would not likely be of much help to the readers and would not bring foreign currency into the country with book sales. However, in a free market, we are each free to do what we do best, what we are best suited for, and what we love. The entire group benefits by being able to read a book that is both well written and well edited.

Why haven't I ever heard any of this before?

I practice evidentiary economics. Economics is a quest for the most efficient use of resources. Evidentiary economics approaches this problem by seeking evidence of what works best. While that may seem obvious, many so-called economic discussions revolve around what some wish the most efficient practices were rather than examining the evidence to substantiate their beliefs. Evidentiary economics examines the evidence to discover methods that maximize benefit and minimize cost. This approach applies to individual, local, and national choices. Evidentiary economics differs from philosophical economics. The John Lennon song "Imagine" might best characterize philosophical economics. Lennon, as talented as he was, had not studied economics. The song's title explains his point of view; he imagines a world that does not exist—a world with no countries, no religion, no possessions, a world where everyone lives for today. Is Lennon's imaginary world better than this one? Who knows? However, what I do know is proposed economic solutions designed for a mythical world cannot help us become more efficient in using resources in the real world.

Evidentiary economics begins with the premise that human beings, like all organisms, are motivated to a great extent by self-interest. Of course, it's okay to imagine we were otherwise and dream Utopian dreams, but people are people, and thousands of years of human history prove just how strong the motivation to benefit the self is.

The Greek philosopher Plato, writing in *The Republic* in 375 BC, may have been the first to employ philosophical economics. Plato thought philosopher-kings, controlling collectively owned property, would be the ideal form of economics and government. However, almost immediately after Plato proposed it, his pupil Aristotle (usually credited as the originator of formal logic) was one of the first to point out that Plato's collectivist ideas failed on logical grounds. Unfortunately, that hasn't stopped people from trying and repeatedly failing to find a way to make philosophical economics work.

Since we've never tried collectivism here in the United States, how do we know it won't work?

Collectivism was actually the first system the early colonists tried. Some of the first European settlers in North America were the pilgrims who came over on the *Mayflower* to settle in Plymouth. They began their settlement as a collectivist enterprise, but it failed—just as all collectivist schemes attempted before and since. The pilgrims had to abandon collectivism to avoid starvation. Only after they reintroduced private ownership and labor did they succeed.

The leader of the colony, Governor William Bradford, wrote in his journal, sometimes called *Of Plimoth Plantation*: "Community of property was found to breed much confusion and discontent, and retard much employment which would have been to the general benefit." He continues, "For young men who were most able and fit for service objected to being forced to spend their time and strength working for other men's wives and children, without any recompense. The strong man or the resourceful man had no more share of food, clothes, etc., than the weak man who was not able to do a quarter the other could. This was thought injustice." Also, "the aged and graver men, who were ranked and equalized in labor, food, clothes, etc., with the humbler and younger ones, thought it some indignity and disrespect to them." Furthermore, "as for men's wives who were obliged to do service for other men, such as cooking, washing their clothes, etc., they considered it a kind of slavery, and many husbands would not brook it."[2]

How do philosophical economists convince so many people they are right?

The answer lies in the wording of the ideologues' position. They fight for the notion that all people should be equal. That sounds noble, but the concept is inherently incorrect. All people are not equal; nor should they be. Before you call for me to be beheaded, let me explain. All people should be treated equally in the eyes of the law and the mores of society. However, all people are not equal. There are inborn differences of height, beauty, physical characteristics, suitability for certain activities, intelligence, certain emotional predispositions, and much more. Early developmental differences include formal and informal education, physical training, developed interests like sports and hobbies, and character development. These are differences that are essential to a happy and productive society.

That's not fair, is it?

It's not only fair; it is necessary for survival. Let's take a look at a few exceptional people in their fields: Albert Einstein, Paul McCartney, Marie Curie, Tom Brady, Martin Luther King Jr., Pablo Picasso, Maya Angelou, Elon Musk, Julia Roberts, Dwight Eisenhower, J. K. Rowling, Steven Spielberg, Agatha Christie, and Walt Disney. These folks couldn't be more different. Of course, they should all be equal in the eyes of the law and society, but would we want them to be equal? Would you consider choosing Julia Roberts to replace Eisenhower as supreme commander of NATO in World War II? How about a pop/rock single written, performed, and sung by Einstein? How about a new murder mystery written by Martin Luther King Jr.? Maybe you'd like to see a major motion picture starring Tom Brady and Maya Angelou, written by Pablo Picasso, and directed by Elon Musk. Do you imagine Paul McCartney making profound scientific discoveries or Marie Curie creating loveable cartoon characters? The differences in people are what make humanity work. The same is true in the natural world as well. How long would life exist if there were only identical lions and no other life on earth?

All people being equal is an example of philosophical economics. The concept favors philosophy over evidence. It means no one can be better at anything than anyone else. The differences—the inequality—between people are the driving force of human progress. Should Sony Pictures be forced to pay Julia Roberts and Albert Einstein the same salary for performing in a film in the name of fairness? That would be terribly unfair to Julia Roberts, who has spent decades perfecting her craft. Should the Arizona Cardinals be forced to pay Tom Brady and Pablo Picasso the same salary as the quarterbacks on their football team? Should they disregard the unique talents and gifts of these two individuals and all the years Brady and Picasso invested in their respective careers?

This logical flaw is the core reason communal economies fail. The ideologues proposing these schemes refuse to acknowledge one stubborn fact: No two people are the same. Therefore, they are not equal. Of course, they must have equal rights, legally and societally. Neither the law nor societal systems such as education, public accommodations, public services, and public access should be able to discriminate between them. But in every other respect, we must accept the reality of this inequality.

Evidentiary economics assumes that economic decisions must depend on how people behave rather than how we wish they would. Economic systems must allow human self-interest to advance the common good by allowing competition to get the best from everyone. Whether we like it or not, it's human nature.

But what about children? Wouldn't all that competition hurt their self-esteem?

Philosophical economists apply this idea of equality to children by giving everyone "participation trophies" and pushing to eliminate advanced classes or giving only pass-fail grades. There is nothing wrong with participation trophies. Showing up is crucial to success, but rewarding outstanding performance is equally important. The hurt feelings some experience are more than outweighed by the good done in helping children find their best path. People and society benefit if individuals pursue avenues they are particularly good at. Children can only learn what they do best by comparing themselves with others. The same is true of schoolwork. Students benefit by seeing they get better grades in science than art or succeed more in music class than mathematics. Children robbed of these opportunities are far more likely to make poor career choices and limit their contributions to society.

But shouldn't people have equal value?

Everyone should be viewed equally under the law and in treatment by society. However, even if we could make everyone equal, should we? Try to imagine what that would mean. Equal means identical. Everyone has the same attributes and abilities. Since no one could be better looking than anyone else, we would all have to look alike; since genders couldn't be different, we would all have to be one gender. It would be a world of clones. Since no one could specialize and develop superior talent in one area, we would devolve to the lowest common denominator. The group cannot increase the innate abilities of its members, so it can only hold back those of greater ability from using it. Human progress would slow to a crawl or cease altogether. For each of us to be unique, we must be different, and if we are different, we are unequal.

> **Only society as a whole can assign value to skills and contributions by what the people choose to purchase and create.**

Only society as a whole can assign value to skills and contributions by what the people choose to purchase and create. Polls asking folks to name the people in the public sphere they admire most or who most affected their lives prove this. Those listed by many as most respected or having the most significant effect on their lives include CEOs, actors, politicians, political wives, singers, jurists, gamers, comedians, government figures, journalists, religious leaders, athletes, talk show hosts, activists, musicians, scientists, philanthropists, inventors, entrepreneurs, leaders of nonprofits, models, film/TV directors-producers, writers, and royalty. Since society doesn't uniformly value varied contributions, variety is essential, which requires inequality. This inequality requires choice. And for a society to succeed, every individual should be free to choose what is most important to them.

SUMMARY: What Is Economics?

Economics is about far more than money. Economics is the study of choice. All organisms make choices, and all choices are economic decisions. Economics is based on the ABCs—actions leading to behaviors and driven by choices. At the personal level, economics is about the actions, behaviors, and choices the individual makes. At the community, national, or global level, it is about the combined actions, behaviors, and choices of the group.

Choices come from values, and we all have a unique list of values that define us. Self-interest means being free to pursue one's values, including values like duty, honor, country, helping others, and self-sacrifice. It is not the same as selfishness. Because our lists of values are unique to the individual, no one is capable of making a decision for someone else.

Evidentiary economics is based on evidence, and philosophical economics is based on a mythical ideal of how the world should be. The evidence shows that societies based on capitalism deliver greater good to more people than societies based on government control of economics and therefore choices.

All people must be equal in the eyes of the law, but we must acknowledge that no two people are equal in every other respect. Any attempts to compel equality in any other respect will diminish all individuals and undermine society. We must recognize our differences are a strength that will create a successful society.

In CPEs, the individual values (choices) of the people are ignored and replaced by the government's values (choices). In capitalism, the values of the people drive the economy. The people vote on what gets made and sold by choosing what to buy. The people's choices overrule the government's choices.

The labels we use (individualism versus collectivism) portray the opposite of reality. Individualism leads to the most successful and harmonious form of social cooperation and brings people together. The ideas of collectivism ultimately lead to resentment and social discord. In most of the places collectivism has been tried, it so divided the people that the result was civil war.

One of the reasons socialism struggles is because socialism is ultimately the attempt of a few to impose what they believe are the "correct" values on everyone else for their own good. They subscribe to Marx's idea of the dictatorship of the proletariat, which is, by definition, the few controlling the many. However, perception of what is good for the group, even a very small group like a family, is difficult; for larger groups, it is impossible. So control of the group by the few always fails to achieve "good" for the many. To be fair, I do think that many socialists—maybe even most socialists—truly believe their solutions will help people. However, it is arrogant and condescending to suggest that anyone knows what is "best" for others.

[3]

What Is Value?

Since economics is the study of choices, where does value come from?

Choice leads to negotiation and compromise, which leads to the concept of value. Most people think of value as being a property of things. While some things are more valuable than others, the value is not an innate property of the things. It's a result of how people think about them. Remember the hay and the cow? What is the value of a bale of hay to a cow? Well, the bale that's one hundred feet away is more valuable to the cow than the one five hundred feet away. That's why it chooses the closer one. The cow must have calories to live, but the cow also values availability. The cow will find the most accessible supply of the calories it demands. All living things ultimately base value on supply and demand. Among humans, these factors interact far more complexly than with lower organisms. Each of our sets of values is as unique as our DNA; no two are alike.

But don't some things have real value, like gold?

Despite its allure, gold has no intrinsic value. It's simply a hunk of metal. Its value is a product of human perception. People are drawn to it. Gold possesses unique and useful properties, and its availability is limited. Consider this: All the gold in the world could be contained within eighteen average American homes. Now, envision a scenario where a 140-mile-wide asteroid—like Psyche, estimated to contain iron, nickel, and gold with a value of about ten quintillion dollars at today's prices—breaks up in our atmosphere. This event would introduce seventy-five thousand times the total value of the entire world's economy in iron, nickel, and gold. Take this headline: "Asteroid Being Captured by NASA Worth $10,000,000,000,000,000,000 Would Make Everyone on Earth a Billionaire"; it suggests that such an event would make everyone on Earth billionaires.[1] However, this perspective fails to grasp the fundamental principles of economics. Let's say Psyche scatters trillions of one-ounce gold nuggets all over the world, thereby multiplying the gold supply on Earth by tens of thousands. Psyche has littered everyone's backyard with gold. How do you think this would affect the value of gold? It could potentially plummet to a point where people would pay others to clean it out of their yards.

The value of everything is "real," but it is set by human desire, not by some innate quality it possesses.

Our desire for goods and services is directly linked to their availability. As the supply goes up—as in the previous example of gold littering everyone's backyards—our desire for it goes down. It might be handy for some things to have that much gold available, and people might still value it for its beauty, but its monetary value would undoubtedly drop dramatically, and indeed, many would pay to have it cleaned out of their yards. The value of everything is "real," but it is set by human desire, not by some innate quality it possesses. Pretty much any material exists in considerable quantities in the universe, but it's like the bale of hay that is five hundred feet away; the effort to get it is not worth what we would gain by having it. Even pure gold is valued differently by different people in the monetary sense. Gold bars with fancy designs sell for 10 percent more than plain gold bars for the same weight of gold. Some folks are willing to pay 10 percent extra to get prettier ones. Some people don't care what they look like and shop for the cheapest gold bars. We all have different values.

What about necessities like food, clothing, or shelter? Doesn't everyone value those the same?

This is a question that challenges our societal perceptions of value and prompts us to think critically about our consumer choices and how they affect value. Do you buy food only for its nutritional value? No, of course you don't. Some people go to the store and buy only generic or store brands. Other people buy only more expensive organic food. And then you have those who buy lots of less expensive, highly processed foods—while others avoid highly processed foods as much as possible. Most people are somewhere in between. Some people only eat at restaurants and are happy to pay others to do the work of cooking the food for them. If you cook it yourself, a quarter-pound hamburger might cost $1.50 or so in 2024, but some fast-food places charge as much as $10 for the same burger, and restaurants can charge $100 or more. They all have approximately the same nutritional value, proving that more than nutritional value affects the price, as the perceived value depends on each individual.

As for clothing, an online search in 2024 found that the value of a pair of jeans varied from a Field & Forest brand pair for $9.99 to a Dussault Apparel variety for $250,000. Both pairs are equally serviceable as clothing, but some people are willing to pay 25,000 times more to get something that goes beyond simply covering up. Wristwatches can go from $10 to tens of thousands; they all tell the time. As for shelter, land in the United States can sell for as little as $50 per acre, and tiny homes start at about $10,000. So for $10,050, you can own a home on an acre of land. Or you can buy an average house on a quarter acre in San Francisco for a little over $1 million. Manhattan townhouses can easily cost $10 million with no land at all; some get to ten times that much. Some mansions in Los Angeles can cost $200 million. So, what is the true cost of shelter? Does $200 million keep you warmer and dryer than $10,050?

What about nonmaterial things? Isn't health the most important thing?

Indeed, some would say so. Others might say community; others might say family. The answers vary because of our individual choices. Look at all the people who eat junk and never exercise—clearly health is not their top value. And many people live more isolated lives because they want to avoid community. Still others choose to reject family.

How we value material and nonmaterial things is affected by our upbringing, our religious and ethical views, the customs we follow, the beliefs and behaviors of those around us, our habits, our ideas of beauty, and much more. Try doing an internet search on the ten most important values, and you will get a vast diversity of answers. Number one on one list may not even be on the next list you find. If you get ten random lists and put them all together, you will probably find fifty different entries on this combined list.

What about human life? Isn't that the most valuable?

That may be true in the Western world today, but its value was far lower in many other times and places. In the not-so-distant past, people thought of human life as cheap. Of course, people still valued their friends and family, but death, serious illness, and injury were commonplace. This lower value led to every region on earth practicing slavery, brutality, and vicious warfare practices at one time or another.

Today, in the United States, we value human life more than any culture in the past has valued it and a great deal more than even many other current cultures. We don't see death and suffering daily the way our ancestors did. In the past and in different parts of the world today, it was/is not uncommon to sell your children into slavery or as property. In North Korea, during the famine in the 1990s, people were afraid and careful because other people were kidnapping children to eat. There were reports of parents eating their own children. In North Korea at that time, life was cheap. People saw death every day and just hoped that their loved ones were not next. Children and their parents were sometimes killed by the state or put in labor camps for watching smuggled-in Western movies or TV shows.

However, we must recognize that we base our feelings about the value of human life on present-day America's values. What some would call repulsive is, of course, correct for our time and place, but historians call that "presentism," a form of bigotry that judges past cultures according to today's mores. People in the past lived in a different world than we do, and that changed what they valued and how much they valued it. You and I weren't raised in that world, so we're in no position to pass judgment on them.

Nothing has innate value. All value results from our choices, and this concept is critical to understanding economics. Most, if not all, economic misunderstandings come from misunderstanding value. Socialists subscribe to the labor theory of value, a significant error. This theory holds that value is derived from labor and labor alone. Marx thought that things that had no material value were a distraction that kept people from focusing on labor. For example, he thought people used religion, like opium, to relieve their suffering caused by the oppression of an unfeeling world. In his ideal world, everyone would contribute all of their talents and abilities to the use of society as a whole, and everyone would take from society whatever they needed. Marx popularized the socialist mantra, the notion of taking from each according to his ability and giving to each according to his need.

Would that be such a bad thing?

That is a value question. We all have different values. I recognize that some may value that concept, and it is not my place to judge what others value. Some people might think it's good. Others might think it's terrible. Marx valuing a world like that is not wrong. He's free to value whatever he pleases; however, putting that idea into practice poses a plethora of problems.

First, who should do the deciding? The individual, society, or the state? For example, if I am a tall person with a good voice, should I be made to play basketball, sing, or work in the salt mines? Marx would say the state (or government) should do the deciding for me. Marx believed that government should match people with professions that serve the state, rather than allowing individuals to pick their own vocations to serve themselves.

Marx thought nonmaterial needs such as art, religion, music, leisure, and the like were distractions, not needs. In a socialist society, like the one he envisioned, material goods should be treated differently. Instead of letting the people decide what their needs are, the government decides what material goods such as televisions and radios, clothing, and the like you have access to. Marx thought everyone should have the same stuff, but I don't see how it is possible. Do you think society, a committee, or a government official should make a list of values and say everyone should get these things in this order, no more, no less?

Socialists, like Marx, would force you to take goods you did not want at the expense of others you wanted. Is that "ideal world" really a perfect world? Also, countries that have tried systems like that quickly developed an illegal black market so people could trade what they had and didn't want for things they didn't have and wanted. If they got caught, the penalties were harsh. It seems more sensible that if we all have different values, we should all have the opportunity to find ways to pursue our unique values rather than anyone else's.

Harvard psychologist David McClelland's research, published in *The Achieving Society*, indicates that achievement is the primary human motivator.[2] Another psychological term often used is *self-actualization*, which refers to working to realize your full potential. According to psychologist Abraham Maslow, self-actualization is the ultimate human need that all people strive for, though few achieve it. I would describe Marx's ideal as societal actualization, or putting into practice the dictates of society as represented by government—a government that decides what values should be actualized and worked toward, not the individual. No one is allowed to achieve their full potential or to self-actualize in a society that is designed to actualize for you.

Achievement or self-actualization often leads to a common misunderstanding. Many folks confuse the monetary reward with the achievement itself, since they both often lead to wealth. But it's the achievement we admire, not the resultant wealth. Self-actualization leads to achievement, and achievement leads to fulfillment and happiness. Whereas societal actualization—the group choosing what goals an individual should pursue—would seem to have the effect of making everyone equally miserable.

That has been the result everywhere it has been tried. It should be evident that no one has the capability to decide what would make someone else happier or better off. Try this experiment: Think of five close friends or extended family members. Are you all the same religion? Do you all own identical vehicles? Do you do all the same activities? Do you all like the same music? Would you be happier if the government forced you to have what they have, do what they do, and live how they live? Would they be happier if the government forced them to live as you do? Think of all the gifts you have received for Christmas or birthdays. How many times did the giver succeed in giving you something you valued for itself rather than as an expression of their love for you? Even your closest friends and family who know and love you most often don't know what you value.

Marx and other socialist theorists think they can devise a list of values everyone agrees on. Like many socialist ideas, it assumes they can do the impossible. Making a list acceptable to two people would be hard enough—ask any married couple. Making a list for the country is simply a foolish notion. Socialists have convinced many people it will work because socialist economists have developed a pleasant-sounding but unworkable theory to use as bait. Then, they used all the false advertising techniques to convince noneconomists that their ideas would work. The only people ever to get rich from socialism are the socialist economists and their political allies in the power elite. The socialists have sold you a lie, and I'm hoping to show you the truth.

How do we apply self-actualization to a national or world economy?

Great question! Once we accept that we all have different values, the idea of a free market as the only fair and reasonable economic system begins to make sense. If you have something higher on your list than mine and I have something higher on my list than yours, it is in both our best interests to trade. That is the basis of the free market. If we're at dinner and you like bread better than salad, and I like salad better than bread, it makes sense to swap my bread for your salad. That is the basis of trade and markets—what most people think of when they think of economics.

Understanding economics is impossible without understanding that we all have different values, and that allows us to help each other by trading. If we all had the same values, we wouldn't have a reason to trade, and we would all be stuck with whatever we had. Trading based on our differing values has no winners and losers, only winners. It might be true that the menu price of the salad is greater than the menu price of the bread, but that doesn't matter because you got the salad you wanted, and I got the bread I wanted. We both won. A socialist would try to convince you that I cheated you because of the difference in menu price, but it's a false premise. How is it possible to cheat someone in a mutually agreed exchange? This lack of understanding of trade based on values rather than menu price, an external valuation, is another of socialism's flawed assumptions.

The earliest humans were basically self-sufficient. Generally, the only specialization that occurred was male and female roles; though not absolute, it most often happened that way. As families evolved into tribes, these early humans found that some people were better at certain tasks than others. For example, Oog was a better hunter, Looha made the best baskets, Guur could find the best edible plants, Houm knew the best medicinal herbs, and so on.

These people learned that the tribe would do better if everyone did what they did best and shared it with the others. People became specialists. As the size of the tribe grew, they found that simple sharing didn't work very well. People squabbled about how to share. Everyone tended to overvalue their contribution and minimize that of others. Also, some people cheated. They didn't contribute their fair share. Of course, this is natural because Oog didn't know about basketmaking, so Oog couldn't appreciate Looha's work. And Looha didn't understand the effort and risks Oog expended in hunting. Oog had to decide how many baskets equaled a pound of venison, and Looha had to do the same. Then, they negotiated and found a compromise. People learned to specialize in skills they enjoyed doing and could perform better than others.

Is there a downside to having less government intervention?

Not all government intervention is bad. For example, some people, such as criminals, lack values that keep them from harming others. In this instance, government involvement is beneficial. The most crucial role of government is to protect its citizens from domestic and foreign threats; to defend citizens' lives, liberty, and property; and to prevent the country from becoming a failed state.

Society progresses most and fastest when everyone pursues their own talents and values. What would be the downside if everyone were free to pursue their values without harming others? Some would say inequality is a downside, and inequality is undoubtedly a result of pursuing different paths. But different values demand different outcomes. There will be those who value money most of all, and so they will give up other rewards to gain wealth. There will be those who value family first, and they will forgo other pursuits to grow a family. There will be those who value music above all and will sacrifice wealth and family to play music.

> **In an ideal free-market capitalist society, everyone is treated equally by the law, viewed as equals by society, and equally happy with their free choices.**

These are choices, and when people are truly free to follow their choices, everyone will be equally happy with their lives. Forcing everyone to be equal in any other way only ensures everyone will be equally unhappy. People should have legal and social equality, but the most important freedom is the freedom to pursue happiness equally. The end result of free-market capitalism is that every member of society can be equally happy but equally unequal in every other respect, except for being equal in the eyes of the law and in the eyes of society. In an ideal free-market capitalist society, everyone is treated equally by the law, viewed as equals by society, and equally happy with their free choices.

If that is true, why hasn't it happened that way?

It hasn't happened that way for two reasons. The first is due to action or inaction by the government. It includes the interference of government in people's choices, the lack of government policing of white-collar criminals manipulating aspects of the market, and corrupted capitalism in which bad actors enlist government help in gaining a competitive advantage over others.

The second reason is there is a need for more public understanding of free markets. Socialist-leaning activists and officials who try to gain power by convincing people the "greedy capitalists" are holding them down have fostered much of this misunderstanding. When people hear that kind of talk enough, they become disempowered and no longer believe their choices matter. The socialists argue they are doing this to make the people's voices heard. That argument is nonsense.

Voices don't matter; choices do. For example, many people today voice their concerns about the prevalence of imports from China but continue to choose to buy Chinese products. Their voices say one thing, but their choices say another. The market, and ultimately people in general, respond to choices, not voices. If someone says they love you but chooses to hurt you, react to the choice, not the voice. Earlier, we discussed the economics ABCs—action, behavior, and choice. I'm sure you've heard the saying "Actions speak louder than words." Actions are the result of choices. Behavior is a pattern of consistent actions that result from consistent choices. So, when we say actions speak louder than words, we are essentially saying choices speak louder than words.

There is often a disparity between voices and choices. Because talk is cheap, literally. It costs nothing to give voice to an idea or a cause, but there is always a cost to choices. In the example of Chinese imports, it costs nothing to complain, but choosing to abstain from those Chinese imports would mean difficulty finding products and more expense for the ones found. If everyone complaining about Chinese imports stopped buying them, new choices would appear worldwide almost immediately. The only reason it has yet to happen so far is because China can make many items cheaper, partly by lowering quality and partly because of a lower-paid workforce.

What about the value of work? Don't people have a right to a living wage?

The value of labor is no different than the value of anything else. Economics, as a scientific discipline, does not attempt to judge value. As we've discussed, value comes from individual choices. As an economist, I have no business telling folks how they should choose. Economics can help people determine the best methods of actualizing their choices but has nothing to say about the choices themselves.

Think of economics like a map. On the map, you can see all the possible destinations. The map doesn't tell you which destination to choose, but it shows you the ways you can get there. Different destinations require different routes, and routes are not created equal. A slow scenic drive along a quiet country lane, a trip through city traffic to the theater, and a hike up a fourteen-thousand-foot peak in Colorado are very different experiences. They have different costs and rewards. Only a fool or a devil tries to impose their version of happiness on others. I am neither, so I refuse to make those kinds of value judgments. People do not have a "right" to a living wage. What they do have is a right to offer the service they would like to provide and to see how valuable that service is to others. If the potential customers don't value the service provided highly enough to result in a "living wage," then the seller needs to improve the service or change to a different one.

The workers ultimately control all jobs. While employers can choose who they want to hire and under what conditions, the workers can choose where to work. But the value of those jobs, like the value of anything, is under the control of the consumer. You and only you, as a consumer, decide how much of your labor you are willing to trade for any commodity. No one has the power, and never should have the power, to force you to spend more of your labor to purchase goods and services at prices higher than their value to you. Only your unique, personal list of what you value first, second, third, and so on should be the standard for the value of things to you. This freedom of choice only exists in free markets, and free markets can only exist with the investment of capitalists. Everyone deserves the right to choose what is in their best interests, how they interact with their world, and what they value. Their choices, not their voices, create a thriving economy.

SUMMARY: What Is Value?

In this chapter we learned that value is the result of community choice. The combined individual value is brought together by how people choose to spend their resources, their time and money. Nothing has intrinsic value—not gold, not diamonds, not services. The only source of value is in the combined lists of values all the members of the community have inside themselves. This applies to all things: food, clothing, shelter, health—even human life. The individual values each of us has is what can lead us to self-actualize and to achieve great things. This leads to specialization and trade, and trade can only function in free markets.

The socialist phrase—from each according to his ability, to each according to his need—displays an incredible ignorance of economics and human nature. No one—least of all a totalitarian socialist state—can effectively replace self-actualization with societal actualization. Nor can it decide what each individual's needs are.

If we apply what we know about human nature and economics, we see that if self-actualization is applied to a national or world economy—each individual choosing their own path—the only viable result is an ideal free-market capitalist society, in which everyone is treated equally by the law, viewed as equals by society, and equally happy with their inherently unequal but free choices.

If you are leaving this chapter a bit confused, that's a good sign. Confusion is a symptom of learning, and I hope you're learning that value choices are complex. Any confusion you may be experiencing is the first step in acquiring and assimilating new knowledge.

[4]

What Is the Economic Value of Labor?

Why can't we raise the minimum wage to $15 per hour for all states?

Why $15 per hour? Why not $20 or $30 or $1,000? Why have a minimum at all? Why not set all wages at $1,000 per hour? What would happen if we set the price of anything? Setting prices or wages is, by definition, fascist—the government controlling the means of production. That has yet to prevent supposed free-market countries from doing so.

I was in Washington during the stagflation in early 1971, hired to aid a recently elected member of Congress who was sworn in that January. I started in mid-February. On my first day, I was walking through a Capitol corridor and happened to fall in step next to someone who looked familiar. I was walking and reading a policy brief when I saw a group of reporters with cameras and microphones blocking the way. I kept approaching them and slowed along with the man beside me. A reporter extended a microphone toward the man next to me after saying, "Are you going to 'jaw-bone' me, Mr. Secretary?" As it happened, the man next to me was John Connally, the newly confirmed Secretary of the Treasury. I stood there trying to look like I knew what was going on as the Secretary had a brief, informal press conference. The unexpected-ness of this situation was not lost on me, and needless to say, my friends and family were astonished that I was on the national news on my first day. The term *jawbone* was Connally's Texas-speak for his plan to avoid wage and price controls by persuading compa-nies and unions to hold off wage and price increases voluntarily. The plan didn't work as well as he'd hoped, and the administration ultimately instituted wage and price controls.

Why shouldn't the government set prices or wages?

Having read this far, you understand that the individual values of consumers set that value. Setting value artificially, by any means, robs consumers of their right to place value. This theft of con-sumers' rights causes distortions in the market; it unintentionally changes consumers' buying habits, which causes changes in pro-duction. That is, consumers and producers find new ways to satisfy consumer demand. These new ways are unpredictable and create market instability. Have you ever gone to the store to buy a favor-ite product and found it out of stock? You probably purchased an alternative instead. Consumers often prefer this alternative to their old favorite, so they keep buying it and stop purchasing their previous favorite. This change in spending produces a permanent reduction in purchasing, which causes a decrease in production because of the lower demand. The same result happens in the presence of wage and price controls.

Obviously, artificially inflated labor costs raise prices. The rise is artificial because a corresponding increase in value does not accompany the price increase. Some say $15 is reasonable because that is the lowest livable wage, and no one should have to work and not make enough for a good life. However, while an increased wage would result in increased consumer cost, there is a more important reason: the idea of value. Of course, everyone is valuable, but the values of everyone's contribution to society can be quite different. One of the most significant economic misunderstandings is about work. Work doesn't necessarily get you anything. You can spend all day digging holes and filling them up again, and you will have done a great deal of work but accomplished nothing. Why not? Because you created no value. Nothing was made better. We say we work for a living, but that's wrong. We actually create value for a living. When the free market is free, we are all guided by the market to find our economic niche—the place where we can specialize in a field where we enjoy creating value. Specialization is what drives human progress. Wage and price controls restrict the market and slow that progress.

We learned thousands of years ago that division of labor benefited society more than complete self-sufficiency. You've heard the phrase "jack of all trades, master of none." If everyone does everything themselves, no one gets exceptional at anything. Think of the famous people we discussed earlier. If they had to build their own houses, fix their own plumbing, and create all their own appliances, they wouldn't have had time to make their contributions to society.

Society progresses much faster when people become experts. Without the division of labor, there would be no brain surgeons, rocket scientists, great musicians and artists, and no one to design next-generation products. These require specialists. Society benefits when everyone finds a niche that takes their talents and abilities to the highest level possible. Free markets allow every individual to find their place in the market by providing every member of society with the most valuable services that an individual can currently offer. Paying a *living wage*, artificially determined, lulls workers into staying in less rewarding jobs instead of growing their talents and abilities and flourishing.

People are different, and all kinds of people have made significant contributions to society in various ways. However, since people are different, they must expect different outcomes. However, everyone should be encouraged to explore their choices and find something they love to do that creates value for others. However, some creations will have more value than other ones, and we value many things that are not the result of labor.

Is this where Marx got it wrong?

In *Das Kapital*, Marx rehashes the *labor theory of value*, which asserts that all value comes from labor. But he was wrong about this central premise of his theory. He had a naive view of the world and failed to acknowledge that people value many things that have nothing to do with labor. For example, we value our families, friends, nature's beauty, exercise, problem-solving, achievements, and so forth. Furthermore, products resulting from the equal time input clearly do not produce equal results. Does it make sense to value the *Mona Lisa* the same as a middle schooler's art project that took the same amount of time to create? The Beatles wrote several of their hit songs in only a few hours. Would it be reasonable to conclude that anyone spending an afternoon writing a song deserves to have a hit record? What about goods that increase in value over time with no additional labor: artwork, some jewelry, wines and spirits, or classic cars? I'm sure the reader can think of many more reasons why this theory makes no sense.

The first important principle to understand about value is that we all have our unique list of how much everything in our life and the world around us is worth, and our list differs from everyone else's. That's one of the reasons socialism struggles: Marx or anyone who believes that the most competent person or government on Earth is smart enough to make those choices about values for anyone else is deluded. Only the individual can decide what is best for themselves and what it is worth to them.

How does seeing value this way provide a different view of the national economy?

First and most importantly, the best action we can take to help individuals and society is to teach people to stop thinking of work and start thinking of creating value. Thinking of your career as work leads to a misapplication of your skills and, therefore, lowers pay and job satisfaction. We currently educate people primarily using a one-size-fits-all litany of facts and formulas. What if instead we helped people in their education to explore and find what they love doing that they want to get especially good at? What if we taught them that by learning to do something they loved, they could have their own best life and serve others by creating something of value for them?

Since our education system doesn't teach people this way, we must find ways to help them from where they are now. Let's imagine someone, Lynn, working at a fast-food joint, Big Burger. Lynn doesn't like spending all day cooking burgers and fries, but Lynn does it anyway, day in and day out, because that's the job. What if Lynn started thinking about creating value? What if Lynn thought about the end customer? So Lynn begins thinking about how to best create customer value. The customers come here because they are too busy to cook or not as skilled as Lynn at making meals. So they are paying Lynn to do it for them. Now, Lynn focuses on providing the maximum value possible for the customer. Lynn will begin moving up in the organization. If Lynn stays focused on delivering outstanding value for the customer, Lynn will soon become a manager and, later, maybe a franchise holder. Someday, Lynn might own Big Burger, much like the incoming CEO of Costco, Ron Vachris, who started there as a forklift operator decades ago. That's how businesspeople succeed; they create the best value for their customers.

Too many people think that business owners are just exploiting the workers. The workers do the work, and the owners take the profit. That's another of Marx's fundamental misconceptions. Most businesses do not set value. Businesses are middlemen. The job of a middleman is to bring consumers and producers together. At Big Burger, Lynn is the producer, the hungry customer is the consumer, and Big Burger is the middleman. Big Burger built the building where the exchange occurs, bought the equipment, paid for employee training, and paid for the raw materials—the burgers and buns. For spending that money to arrange the exchange between producer and consumer, they take part of the profits. Without this middleman, there would be no exchange, Lynn would be out of a job, and Lynn's customers would stay hungry.

But Big Burger doesn't set the price; it discovers it. They can't charge more and pay Lynn more. Because Big Burger doesn't decide the value, the consumer—or, more correctly, the collection of all possible consumers—decides what it's worth to them not to have to cook today. If the price goes above their set value, they won't eat at Big Burger; they'll go home and cook their own or go to Cheap, Cheap Chicken instead. If many consumers decide that way, Big Burger will have to start laying off producers because if Big Burger has more producers than consumers, the business of bringing producers and consumers together fails. Part of the middleman's job is to monitor prices and set the prices at the point that brings together the most producers and consumers. Big Burger makes more profit this way, which means more producers and consumers benefit. As a result, everyone wins!

If Big Burger can't charge more, can't they just take less profit and still pay Lynn and their other employees more?

Another socialist fallacy. Setting up a Big Burger is expensive and risky. If someone is going to invest a few hundred thousand dollars to build something with a 1-in-4 chance of failing in three or four years, they will have to earn more than for a lower-risk investment. Typical restaurant profit margins are 3–5 percent. Certificates of deposit can earn as much as 2.5 percent with no risk. If investments don't reward people for taking significant financial risks, they won't take them. Those risks are necessary for Big Burger to exist and for Lynn to have the opportunity to create value.

But why should the company get more of the profits if the employees are doing all the work?

Some argue the company's owners aren't doing any work to make that money. But that's not true. They worked for the money they were putting at risk by creating Big Burger, and their profits are fair compensation for investing in employment opportunities for others. In addition, most restaurateurs, like most business owners, have to work twelve to fifteen hours daily. They usually work longer hours than their employees and don't get any overtime.

Most entrepreneurs work exceptionally hard and are trying their best to create value by doing something they love. Most restaurant owners put in very long hours. They love their restaurants and seeing people enjoy their food. Most of their employees don't share their passion, unfortunately. They don't delight in customers appreciating the staff's efforts as they do, and they don't put in as many hours—and the few employees who do have the passion end up leaving and starting their own establishments.

> **Most entrepreneurs work exceptionally hard and are trying their best to create value by doing something they love.**

Doesn't work have inherent value?

Trying to set wages is based on the belief that things have intrinsic value. But nothing has inherent value, including work. Work, goods, ideas, and so on only have value for those who value them. When many people value something, and it's in limited supply, its price rises. That's how supply and demand works.

Take gold. Gold is valuable because many people want it and it is in short supply. According to the USGS, we know of 244,000 metric tons of gold on Earth.[1] If you do the math, that means that all the gold we know of would fit in a warehouse cube seventy feet on a side. We all value the air we breathe, but at least for the time being, it's not in short supply, so it has low monetary value. Garbage, on the other hand, has negative economic value. It's in plentiful supply, but no one wants it, so we pay people to take it away.

Like the air we breathe, any given person may not be in such great demand that they have high monetary value. Our monetary value is in the value we can create. A person with skills in short supply and high demand will have higher monetary value than someone with easy-to-find skills in low demand. Those clamoring for a higher minimum wage scream, "That's not fair!" but that's another socialist presupposition that makes no sense. It is a part of human existence; you are free not to like it, but the concept is unchangeable.

People value what they value. Socialists believe that people, like animals, could be trained to have different values. One value most people hold is freedom, and every time governments have tried to take away that freedom, they have eventually failed, because the government was unable to train people to enjoy living without freedom. A critical part of freedom is the freedom to assign your unique value to things and labor. The value you assign is a particular part of being you. You will never find another person with precisely the same values. And that's wonderful!

I have a friend, Pat, who loves to make jewelry but is upset that selling the jewelry doesn't make enough to live on. I've tried to talk to Pat about it with little success. Does anyone make a good living selling jewelry? Of course they do. Pat may not be very good at it or lack marketing skills and could benefit from hiring an agent. My friend may have also yet to study what people like in jewelry. Many artists, musicians, and artisans, like jewelry makers, believe in art for art's sake. They make what they value and think is beautiful, and that's great! But if you want to sell your art, it must have value for others. For this to happen, you have to create what others want to buy. Some call that selling out, and you could call it that, but if you want others to want to purchase your products, you have to create ones they like. Socialists have, as a part of their belief system, the idea that if they or the government tell them they must like one thing over another, they will submit and do so. How well would that work with you? Could the government change your values?

If so, maybe I'm wasting my time writing this book. If all socialists like things because someone tells them to, I could simply tell them to like free markets and capitalism and be done with it. We both know that won't work because socialists, like everyone else, don't like things because someone tells them they should.

Should we have to please others to make a living?

Indeed, you don't. Why do the Beatles have more hits than the Grateful Dead? Do Beatles songs have greater intrinsic value than Dead songs? No. By now you know that nothing has inherent value. The Beatles have more hits than the Grateful Dead because more people enjoy their songs. It doesn't mean their songs are better. It simply means more people enjoy Beatles music over the Grateful Dead. As a result, they hold more value to more people. The Grateful Dead didn't strive to please as many people as the Beatles, but I believe they were content with their choice. The freedom to create value is a potent tool that can pave the way to success and happiness. It's a beacon of hope and liberation.

Several states and cities have raised the minimum wage to $15 per hour, so why all the fuss? The world didn't end.

No, the world didn't end, but it made life much more challenging for many of society's most vulnerable. Have you noticed that many retail stores are installing self-checkout lanes? That's a direct result of the increase in the minimum wage. To keep prices at a point where consumers keep buying, they must find alternatives to higher labor costs. One of the groups of workers harmed by the minimum wage laws that some states have adopted is supermarket checkers.

Self-checkout lanes replace checkers as quickly as cities and states enact those laws. Some say we should all refuse to use those self-checkout lanes because they are job killers. However, if the idea is to preserve or create jobs, then in addition to taking out the self-checkout lanes, why not also take out the scanners the checkout folks use and make them enter each purchase by hand? That would probably double the number of checkers, but it would substantially increase the price of groceries and the wait time for customers. It's always unfortunate when someone's employment is interrupted, but halting economic progress for the good of one group is not the answer.

Can't we just ban self-checkout lanes and give checkers their jobs back?

If work of any kind is what enables progress, then why not ban every form of labor-saving device? In addition to self-checkout lanes, maybe we should ban the wheel, the computer, electricity, aircraft, hammers, axes, spears, plows, flint arrowheads, and so forth. We could all dig, scrap, and claw with nothing but our bare hands—then everyone would be working just like they were forty thousand years ago. We would have full employment. Is that anyone's idea of the perfect world?

Our goal as an economic society must be for humanity to thrive. The only way that happens is by finding more and better ways to use resources, including time and work, most efficiently. Free markets have repeatedly proven that, combined with capital investment, they provide more benefits to more people than any other method. Furthermore, if you compare per capita GDP over time, progress clearly means that even the poorest person today lives better than anyone did forty thousand years ago; the vast majority live better than the wealthiest did just two hundred years ago, and the average person lives far better than the richest did even a hundred years ago. Life cannot both get better and stay the same.

Change always affects some people negatively, but we can't let that prevent us from moving forward to a better world. The importance of progress and efficiency in the economy cannot be overstated. It is what drives innovation, creates jobs, and improves living standards. One of the alternatives that has driven progress throughout history is mechanization and automation.

You say throughout history, but isn't this relatively new?

That depends on your definition of new. The earliest labor-replacing device that comes to mind is the wheel, somewhere around

15,000 BC. I'm no expert on neolithic economic history, but the invention of the wheel put many travois, drag cart makers, and drag haulers out of work. On the other hand, there was a significant increase in employment for wheel makers.

However, since a wheeled cart allows you to carry more substantial loads farther and faster, there may have been a short-term decrease in drivers. But, as the technology caught on, people could become more mobile, which probably led to increased driver employment. Consider the windmill. Originally, grain was milled by hand and later by rotary mills powered by human muscle. Even later, horse, donkey, and ox power replaced human muscle. Finally, people harnessed the wind to do the work of turning the millstone. That probably caused a good deal of unemployment in the short run, but as usual, it created more employment in the long run in the form of mill designers, builders, and repairers.

Similarly, the printing press surely put many copyists (the folks who copy books by hand) out of work; the steam engine eliminated thousands, maybe millions, of menial labor jobs; railroads put long-haul wagon companies out of business; the mechanical reaper dramatically altered farm labor practices; the internal combustion engine and electricity dramatically changed the labor market; the personal computer destroyed the typewriter and carbon paper industries.

We could keep this up for quite a while, but I'm sure you get the idea. Most of those changes happened long before minimum wage rules, but they represent the attempt to lower labor costs, whatever the cause. However, there are many direct examples as well. Until the 1970s, almost all gas stations had attendants who filled your tank, washed your windshield, and checked your oil. Minimum wage increases forced stations to go to self-serve gas pumps. The customers were unwilling to pay extra for someone else to do the job for them. Most assembly line jobs have had workers replaced by robots. Today, when you call many businesses, a computer tries to answer your questions before connecting you with a living person. Most sorting and packing facilities are also automated. While ultimately beneficial to society, these advancements have all come at a human cost.

What do you mean by a "human cost"?

By *human cost* I mean the impact these advancements will have on others. For example, putting people out of work is not desirable, but it is often necessary to achieve progress. Economists call this *creative destruction*, which is a term that underscores the necessity of change for societal advancement.

People protesting progress is as old as humanity. Look around your house. Every labor-saving device you see costs someone their job. Electricity put an end to whale oil lamps and the whalers and the lamp makers. Your refrigerator bankrupted the ice houses and the icemen they employed. Your dishwasher, washing machine, and dryer meant thousands of household servants lost their jobs. Television and film killed vaudeville and dance halls. As people create new ideas for products, others get destroyed.

Can't we find a way to make progress less destructive?

Honestly, I don't see how. Every product or service is a complex amalgamation of consumer wants and needs. Consumers always want more, better, and different. It's never simple. Consider singer-songwriters. They write their songs and try to find an audience that will pay to hear them. They learn over time what kind of songs people will pay to hear, so they write more songs in that genre. They learn that stage presence makes a difference, so they polish their act. More effective methods replace less effective ones. But they must stay flexible because tastes change, and big bands get replaced by jazz, blues, and country. And those get outpaced by rock and roll, which gives way to heavy metal, only to be replaced by rap and female pop.

All these changes eliminated jobs and put people out of work but created new jobs that employed others. This is the concept of creative destruction, the way society progresses, and it's a fascinating and engaging process to observe despite its adverse side effects. However, when this change happens naturally, without outside interference, it tends to happen much more slowly. This more gradual change gives the folks affected more time to adjust and plan ahead. When it happens because of outside pressure, like government wage controls or union demands, the disruptions happen much more quickly, making it much more difficult for workers to make smooth transitions.

Entrepreneurs experiment with new products all the time. They can attract capitalists to fund their start-up business if their goods and services seem promising. Existing businesses are constantly seeking ways to attract new consumers with better value. Sometimes, these new ideas don't attract the customers as hoped—think the defunct Google Glass or the game *Cyberpunk 2077*—and the business suffers or fails. I think the objections are because creative destruction is not a well-organized, systematic progression toward a known outcome. For better or worse, that's the only way it works because no one knows ahead of time what will attract consumers and what will not. That is part of why socialist planners usually fail. Progress is an experiment in human nature, and consumers must be the final decision-makers.

Actions speak louder than words. Consider the self-checkout available at Walmart and other stores. Some consumers may complain about having to check out their own items when lines are long, but they continue to choose the lower prices for equal quality at these stores that use self-checkout lanes and hire fewer cashiers while passing the savings on to the consumer. It's like what happened with gas station attendants in the mid-1960s and '70s, when self-serve pumps became the norm rather than the exception. In late 1966, as a high school senior, I was forced out of my part-time job pumping gas by the conversion to self-serve gas. Customers decided that rather than pay me to pump gas for them, they'd rather do it themselves for less money (even if it meant there would be fewer gas station attendants and some, like me, would lose their jobs).

What about union workers? They can go on strike, so this is less of an issue for them, right?

While they can go on strike, if the market will not bear the increased wages they seek, US companies will outsource their work to nonunion states or overseas. Possibly the most obvious case of this economic cause and effect involved the International Ladies' Garment Workers' Union (ILGWU). Union action, similar to when the government sets wages, tries to set value artificially, but it never works in the long run. After several successful union strikes, the rising labor costs led garment manufacturers to begin outsourcing to nonunion states or foreign countries. Some of you may remember the TV commercials from 1978–1981 produced by the union, with a jingle asking shoppers to look for the union label on the clothes they buy. Union employment continued to drop, and in 1982, the union held the largest strike in New York City history. This union "success" led to far more outsourcing, and now, the vast majority of women's clothes for the US market are made in nonunion states or overseas. While the catchy jingle may have made consumers look for the label, it also led them to look at the price difference, and consumers chose lower prices.

Union membership in the United States is at an all-time low, with only 14.4 million members or 10.0 percent of the workforce.[2] This is less than a third of the peak union membership in the late 1940s of 34 percent and half of the 1983 level.[3] This reduction is despite high-profile attempts to organize during the last couple of years in several industries. More than half of the current union membership are government employees who don't have to worry about those pesky consumers. Federal employees in those unions are forbidden to strike. As is often the case, the government exempts itself from the rules it makes for others.

This decline in union membership reflects a shift in the labor market and the increasing influence of consumer choice on labor dynamics. Unions make the mistake of thinking they have great power, but they can only exercise that power temporarily since the consumers always win in the long run.

I'm not anti-union. I'm an economist, and I understand the consequences of union activity. Going back to the ILGWU, they effectively improved wages and working conditions for their members, but this temporary gain came at the expense of jobs for the next generation of workers. Unions typically get short-term gains but suffer long-term losses.

If you think that's a good trade-off, then supporting this kind of union activity makes sense, but most union supporters don't see the long-term consequences of their demands. You get more money now, but your kids can't get a job. It's up to you to decide if that's a good trade. I'm not judging. I'm just clarifying the trade. Labor is valued the same way other things are, and attempting to change the value artificially will always fail in the long run. Consumers ultimately decide value, so it's crucial to understand the long-term implications of our choices.

Then what do we do to help people who are struggling to make a living?

I'm glad you asked! The only factor that can raise wages in the long run is increased value productivity. Creating more value in the same amount of time is the way to achieve this goal. Much of the problem exists because our educational system needs to teach people that their job is not to work but to create value. When you were younger, did you think to ask yourself, "What skills and aptitudes do I have—or can I develop—that will maximize my ability to create value in ways that are fun and rewarding for me?" Many college programs are fine for those who want to learn something they're interested in without regard to the potential to create value. Some are obvious, and some are surprising. The obvious ones are those with no related career field.

Gender studies, for example, has no equivalent job title, like genderist. If you study physics, you become a physicist. I have a PhD in economics, and I am an economist. See the difference? Many other degrees only lead to postgraduate work and competing for academic jobs. History, art history, biology, anthropology, archaeology, philosophy, environmental science, and psychology have little to offer those with only a bachelor's degree.

You might be surprised to hear me say this, but economics is in the same category. Becoming an economist usually requires a PhD. That doesn't mean people should only consider what they can do to create the most value. Not everyone wants to be a brain surgeon. The important thing is to plan for enjoyable ways to create value. Most people, sadly, come home after a day's work and can't see the value they created. That's not a fun way to live.

The people most satisfied with their careers enjoy the day-to-day doing of their jobs and get great satisfaction from the value they have created. I have a friend who finished her degree quite a few years ago in English literature, and the only jobs available are in high schools, and very few of those. She doesn't want to teach high school. She fell into the trap of job titles not matching degree titles. There are no jobs for an English literaturist.

I've encouraged her to seek alternate routes. Her degree may not lead directly to a job, but hopefully, she chose that path because she enjoyed studying it. I encourage folks to spend some time thinking about their passions (e.g., activities you'd like to spend each day doing) and then balance that by examining their skill sets and exploring what talents and abilities they have with the potential to create value for others. Part of why my friend chose English literature is because she enjoys reading and writing. Should she consider other applications of those skills? One example would be technical writing—writing manuals for products. A well-written, engaging manual might be a fun challenge that creates a great deal of value. The market for technical writers is excellent and pays well. I'm not trying to convince her to go that route, but it's a good example.

I hate to admit it, but I'm sort of in the same boat. My degree is in political science, and there are very few jobs out there. Do you have any ideas for me?

Your situation may require some volunteer work to get you started. You might try getting involved politically. Start working as a volunteer on political campaigns. Maybe seek out an unpaid opening for a precinct committee member. If you love doing it, you'll probably work harder than most volunteers and, because of your training, do a better job. That could easily result in an entry-level staff position on a campaign, and that could lead to a job on legislative staff and, ultimately, a chance to run for office yourself. But since you're not going to make any money at first, you probably shouldn't quit your day job.

Fair enough, but what if I don't like my day job?

Unfortunately, you aren't alone when it comes to work. Society has done a poor job of helping people learn how to combine creating value with following their bliss. We've taught people they must work for a living, but that's wrong. No one ever gets paid to work; they get paid to create value for others.

Creating value instead of working has several significant effects. Focusing on creating value will likely lead to success in any job or career. If you stop working and start creating value, you will undoubtedly create value more effectively. Focusing on value creation leads to pay raises, promotions, and appreciation. And even though every job creates value, if you can't see your job as value creation, change jobs!

Find a job where you can see value creation. However, you can find value creation in every job. It must be there, or no one would be willing to pay for it. As far as pay goes, to paraphrase the Beatles, "And in the end, the value you take should be equal to the value you make."

> ## Choice is the beating heart of free-market capitalism because we all want different things.

In free-market capitalism, all choices are honored. And choice is the beating heart of free-market capitalism because we all want different things. The business owners' choices, the workers' choices, the artists' and self-employed workers' choices, and the customers' choices all drive the economy. Some businesses will have cashiers, and some will have self-checkouts.

Those who want to control the market by creating a monopoly are choice thieves. They may not intend it that way, but ultimately, their belief that they can set value for all of us is arrogance; we don't need to choose because they know better. Despite the unintended negative consequences, letting the free market decide wages and prices is ultimately the fairest and most beneficial path to progress and a better world for all.

SUMMARY: What Is the Economic Value of Labor?

While the market decides the value of labor, labor is no different than anything else. It has no intrinsic value. The consumer is the sole determiner of value, or rather, the collection of all possible consumers, the market. Setting a minimum wage of $15 per hour or any other amount is the government usurping the customer's and the producer's right to negotiate fair value.

Throughout history, innovation, driven by the consumer's desire for better goods and services at lower prices, has upended people's lives. No one wants to see people have to readjust their lives, but the change happens much more quickly when the government, unions, or any force outside the market interferes. We can make the shift less destructive by letting it happen more slowly and naturally. Automation and other disruptive forms of creative destruction will continue, but these forces move more slowly when outside actors do not push them.

The most effective long-term strategy to avert catastrophic disruptions is education. When individuals comprehend that their financial well-being is directly linked to the value they contribute, they are empowered to make more informed decisions. Seeking opportunities where someone can maximize their value creation is a vastly different approach than simply searching for a job. Viewing the free market as a platform to exchange the value each of us generates, based on our unique talents and priorities, not only enhances individual lives but also cultivates a stronger, more equitable free market for all.

[5]

What Is Trade?

Picking up where we left off earlier in our example of how trading began, Oog traded venison for Looha's baskets, Guur would trade edible plants for Houm's medicinal herbs, and so on. But as the tribes grew more extensive, this system became overly complicated, so they began using objects like shells, special stones, or metals as value tokens—what we would call money today. This use of crude money was the birth of the free market.

Money is a way to simplify trading. Trading with only two people is easy, but it gets complicated when more than two people are involved. It might be doable if we were all in the same room. Otherwise, we need a way to keep track of all the trades. Early cultures initially chose objects that were more accessible, such as stones and shells, to stand for value. Eventually, most cultures began using gold as money, because it is not easy to find in large quantities. Thus, it tends to have a pretty consistent value for a multitude of people.

But wouldn't shells have worked just as well as gold?

No, probably not. Early cultures discovered that using shells had one significant disadvantage. If someone found a secluded beach with tons of shells, they could buy up a lot of goods without trading anything of their own that someone else valued. It's similar to what we would call counterfeiting today. Gold is different. As I said, gold is really hard to find in large quantities. It's scarce.

We don't use gold anymore, though. It got to be a pain to carry around, so people started using what you might call gold certificates. A piece of paper issued by the government was backed by gold, which the government had stored. If you had one of these, you could always trade it back to the government for gold. This system is called the gold standard. From the 1930s through the 1970s, most of the world went off the gold standard and replaced it with fiat money. Fiat money has no "true" value. The government establishes its value by government order or fiat. This shift had profound implications on our economy, shaping the way we understand and interact with money today.

That sounds a little sketchy. How is that different than using shells?

That's exactly right! It's the same concept, and the government has a secret hoard of "shells." I'm sure you've heard people use the phrase "the gold standard" to refer to the best example in its class. That metaphor is used because the gold standard is generally thought to be the best economic policy. However, governments wanted to spend more money than they had in gold. Governments understand that money is a form of power. Thus, the more money they control, the more power they have over the populace.

Today, US government spending is five times greater than it was in 1930. Consequently, the US government has five times the power it had then. Should we assume the government does good things with all that money? Maybe, but for whom? Remember that list of values we all have in our heads? A government can't decide what is best for everyone because we are all different. In addition, when the government controls how money is spent, people with power can steer the government to spend that money in ways that benefit them at the expense of everyone else.

How can we stop the government from doing that?

We need better economics education. The concept of a middleman is something most people need help understanding. Many people mistakenly believe that middlemen are exploiters. But middlemen are essential to a trading economy. Take franchised fast-food shops. They typically cost in the neighborhood of $2 million to set up—the building, the cooking equipment, the furniture, and so on. On average, this investment returns $150,000 per year. That's an annual return on investment of 7.5 percent. A Vanguard or Fidelity S&P fund earns about 10 percent annual average with far lower risk. In addition, franchisees typically work longer hours than the employees and are somewhat more stressed.

Why do we need middlemen? Imagine what a world without them would look like. The job of a middleman is to bring producers and consumers together. Without middlemen, everyone would be self-employed, producing what they could and marketing it themselves. This lack of middlemen is how early economies functioned, but it was very limiting because it's no easy task to find all the potential consumers to sell to.

> **Middlemen matter, because they do the jobs that the producer can't do effectively or would rather not.**

For example, as a writer, I am classified as self-employed, but I rely on a middleman, my publisher, to help craft my work into a more marketable product. Why? Because they know far more than I do about how to bring together the producer and consumer—in this case the writer and the reader. Yes, I could self-publish, but then I'd probably have a product that, without expert editing, expert cover design, and an experienced marketing team, would attract far fewer readers. Middlemen matter, because they do the jobs that the producer can't do effectively or would rather not. This results in better products for consumers and ensures that more customers can benefit from the value created by the producers.

I have a friend who sells handmade jewelry and hats on Etsy and eBay. Isn't that exactly what you're talking about? It works fine for my friend.

Yes, there is no doubt that worldwide marketing by individuals is easier now than ever before in human history, but Etsy and eBay are middlemen. Their creators built the website, handled the advertising, and charged fees to your friend for using their capital investment.

Now, your friend could do what some do and start a website from which to sell products, but now, instead of making jewelry and hats, some of that time will have to be spent making websites or doing other tasks requiring a different skill set. However, some people can do very well that way. It can work well for unique items that can be handmade, but most of the products we use every day have to be made on a much larger scale to be cost-effective.

Furthermore, your friend uses middlemen to obtain the tools and raw materials needed for production. I doubt your friend has a gold, silver, or turquoise mine in their backyard. Does your friend have the know-how and raw materials to build a soldering iron? Does your friend grow cotton and raise sheep to have cotton and wool available to make hats? Does your friend have an oil well and a way to process crude oil into synthetic fabrics?

In reality, your friend uses middlemen when purchasing goods. And when your friend turns these purchased materials into a value-added finished product, your friend has become a middleman. Because your friend can only create relatively simple products on a small scale, your friend must charge customers much more than the same product of equal quality made in a factory. They may be unique, one-of-a-kind creations. While some people will pay the extra premium for something unique, most will not. Your friend also faces a problem of scale. It will be difficult to expand operations as demand increases.

In addition to the economy-of-scale problem, many products require a vast collection of people to manufacture them. Take, for example, the cell phone in your pocket. It has raw materials from dozens of countries, and the design is the combined work of dozens, maybe hundreds of engineers, and its manufacture requires advanced robotics to make chips and circuit boards that no one can make by hand. If you want products requiring advanced manufacturing techniques, you need a middleman who can put it all together.

But that sounds exploitative. If the workers are doing the work, shouldn't they get all the profit?

Capitalism is not exploitative. On the contrary, it has empowered and inspired greatness in individuals—like Steve Jobs, who started Apple in his garage and revolutionized the tech industry, and Jeff Bezos, who started Amazon as an online bookstore and turned it into a global e-commerce giant. Both of these visionaries created tremendous value and wealth for their employees and stockholders, which doesn't sound like exploitation to me.

Tyranny and exploitation require the use of force. No corporation can force anyone to do anything. They may have rules and expectations that they want their employees to adhere to, but the employees are free to go elsewhere if they don't like it there. Only governments can be tyrannical since only they have the power. Capitalism has no power. It has no means to exploit anyone.

If workers want to earn a profit, they will need to go into business for themselves. So, instead of working somewhere like Big Burger and collecting wages, they would have to quit their job and start cooking burgers in their own kitchen. Then they would need to sell them to other customers while competing with more established places like Big Burger who have a built-in customer base, professional kitchen, and line cooks.

Let's pretend for a moment that the government would not interfere in your endeavor. Sounds pretty good, right? Leave Big Burger and sell your own burgers. Then you'd get all the profit (along with all the risk of going into business for yourself). If you don't like your job or think you need to be paid more, you are free to find a better way. That's how free markets work.

Many people, however, prefer the security of working for a middleman who will take the risks and make the investment required to provide others with a way to create value. Yes, they make money doing it, often more money than those who work for them, but that's because they are willing to take the risks and make the investments necessary to create a business—risks the employees choose not to take.

Steve Jobs and Jeff Bezos are just a couple of examples of how capitalism can empower individuals to create value and wealth for millions of employees and stockholders. The wealthy today are not like the wealthy three or four hundred years ago. They are far more likely to be folks like Jobs and Bezos—entrepreneurs who made their money by creating new wealth for everyone rather than living off fortunes built up over centuries by exploiting others.

It seems to me that many negative feelings about the rich are rooted in envy. What do you think?

That's somewhat true. However, much of that envy comes from fixed-pie thinking. In the past, when economies were zero-sum, the rich got their wealth by exploiting others and by inheriting wealth from previous generations who acquired it by exploiting others. As a result, the rich had a reputation for unearned indulgence, resulting in envy.

Don't get me wrong, I'm not suggesting that envy is helpful; it's not. Seeing others doing nothing to possess massive wealth while you are working tirelessly to get by is a situation likely to produce envy. Now, while there are still some who can live opulently on inherited wealth, their numbers are shrinking. More than 80 percent of US millionaires are self-made. In fact, all of the ten wealthiest in the United States are consistently in that category.[1]

Marx says wealth itself causes greed and envy. He says property is the sole cause, and that's why we should do away with private property. Most of Marx's writing indicates a simplistic view of the world. People envy the beautiful, the talented, the intelligent. People envy anything that others have that they wish they had. This multifaceted nature of envy is intriguing. Greed manifests itself not only in matters of property; it includes matters of attention, admiration, power, and, in fact, anything that gives people an advantage over others. People envy not only money but also their neighbors' spouses, power, and position, as we discussed earlier. The world's major religions consider envy a cardinal sin—a moral failure that is the proximal cause of many or all resulting moral shortcomings. So people still envy the rich, not realizing that they are working hard to get what they have and are not like the rich layabouts of old.

Now, some envy the rich's attributes, drive, work ethic, intelligence, or achievements in the same way that they envy rich musicians or athletes. It's no longer the wealth itself that people envy but the achievement. Is that bad? It depends. As we discussed earlier, admiration for the accomplishments of others is a good thing. It only descends to envy if it motivates one to do or wish for something immoral to alter the situation. This distinction between admiration and envy is crucial to understanding the psychological and philosophical implications. If someone dreams about taking someone down a peg because of their legitimate accomplishments, that's envy, and it's a problem.

So, are we now living in an achieving society?

Yes. Harvard psychologist David McClelland's research, published in *The Achieving Society*, explores human motivation and identifies three primary motivators: achievement, affiliation, and power.[2]

His work has been used extensively in business schools to determine how to best motivate employees. All three of McClelland's motivators are intimately tied to status. Marx's ideas about society tend to ignore and actively undermine these motivators. McClelland concludes that societies and subsets of societies could be predicted to be successful if they score high on achievement as a motivator. Marxists believe that what people want is the reward of achievement—money—when what they actually want is the achievement itself. Ideas like social promotion in schools and participation trophies in sports are symptoms of the Marxist belief that the reward is what people crave. These false prizes destroy ambition and work ethic while rewarding the less deserving. Therefore, Marx's focus on property as the source of greed and envy is illogical and detrimental to society.

Having a high school diploma used to mean something. Now, lax standards have dramatically devalued even college degrees. Helping people get the result without the achievement is not helping. The phenomenon is patronizing and undermining. It says, "You aren't worthy of this, but we'll give it to you anyway because we are so magnanimous."

We need to invest in helping folks achieve, not subsist.

That does not mean I'm opposed to public assistance. On the contrary, I'm all for public assistance if it actually assists people in improving their lives. If it means giving them subsistence income without any corresponding steps to solve the underlying problems, then, yes, I'm opposed. We need to invest in helping folks achieve, not subsist. Most who are at the subsistence level are there because they don't have the tools they need to succeed. They might need counseling, job training, rehab, or education. All public assistance should be coupled with programs to enable achievers and should be time-limited.

Speaking of envy, the movie *Wall Street* portrays capitalists as believing greed is good; is it?

The answer is a resounding no. Greed is one of the seven deadly sins. These sins, derived and refined from ancient folk wisdom and early philosophical works, were incorporated into the teachings of the Roman Catholic church in the fourth century. Pope Gregory, in 590, further shaped them into the modern form we know today. Most Christian denominations have since adopted this labeling of these sins, often referred to as the capital vices, as they are believed to be the root of all other vices. The seven sins are pride (false pride or narcissism), greed, wrath (anger or rage), envy, lust (for more than necessary), gluttony (too much eating or drinking), and sloth (laziness).

This isn't going to be a religion lesson, but religions, whether you believe them or not, hold a great deal of collected wisdom. I don't mean just Christianity; Islam and Buddhism have more limited lists of cardinal sins, but greed is on all. A careful examination of the lists reveals that greed may be more fundamental than other sins. Pride is greed for attention or undeserved praise. Greed denied results in anger. Envy is a type of pre-greed or a greed motivator. Lust is greed across a broader range of objects. Gluttony is greed for food or drink. Sloth is greed for an easy life. If envy is pre-greed, envy and the resulting greed may be the "root of all evil." People often misquote the Bible as saying that money is the root of all evil, but what it says is "the love of money is the root of all evil"; the love of money is greed. This blind love of money leads one to do anything for money.

We must understand the distinction between greed and legitimate self-interest. Self-interest is a natural instinct necessary for survival, and all living organisms possess it. Greed, on the other hand, is the desire for more, coupled with the willingness to do anything to get it, often at the expense of others. Wanting to increase financial gain through fair exchange is not greed, regardless of the amount of money involved. If the trade is fair, all parties involved should feel benefited. For instance, a budding entrepreneur who creates a new phone app that millions love and becomes a multibillionaire is not driven by greed. Similarly, the venture capitalist who provides the funds to launch the app and shares in the profits is not guilty of greed.

This reasoning applies to the other sins as well. Consider gluttony as a metaphor for greed. Is eating six large meals a day gluttony? Not if you are an Olympic weight lifter or ultramarathoner. Eating 6,000 calories a day is not gluttony if you are burning 6,000 calories a day, but if you are burning 1,500 calories a day, it's gluttony, particularly if your gluttony leads you to steal from others to obtain more food.

Consider lust as the lust for power. Learning martial arts for sport or self-defense is not lust for power, but learning karate to bully others is. Learning hypnotism to heal with hypnotherapy is not lust for power; hypnotizing people to bend them to your will is. Think a moment about pride. Is it wrong to finish a significant accomplishment and feel proud of yourself for getting it done? No! Is it wrong to make up a false accomplishment and put it on your resume? Yes! Especially if, in doing so, you harm others who deserved the job but didn't get it because of your narcissistic pride. Is false pride or narcissism or putting yourself above others wrong? Yes!

So greed is similar; wanting more rewards—money—by providing others with something of value to them is not greed; cheating them in the deal is.

So greed is placing money over morality?

Yes. The desire for money is not problematic, but wanting money badly enough to be willing to do immoral actions to acquire it is. In Mishna 1:14 of the *Pirkei Avot*, Hillel the Elder describes Jewish philosophy in this way: "If I am not for myself, who will be for me? And if I am only for myself, what am I?" Looking out for one's self-interest is necessary; enriching oneself at the expense of others is wrong.

If you get rich by stealing or cheating from an existing pool of resources, you're doing wrong. But if you acquire wealth by growing the pie, you deserve your wealth because you have enriched everyone. In a fixed-size economy, being wealthy would be greedy because exploiting others was the only way to gain wealth. However, in today's growth economy, the rich acquire wealth with innovation that grows a bigger economy and delivers a bigger, tastier piece of the pie to everyone.

Aren't there still greedy capitalists today?

Of course there are. Greed drives some capitalists to find ways to cheat; it is incumbent on the government to identify and stop them. Are most free-market capitalists greedy? No! Most capitalists and entrepreneurs constantly seek better ways to create products and services the world needs and wants. Every occupation has greedy practitioners; capitalists are no different, but they are no worse, either. Greed is definitely not good. However, there are many greedy people in the world, including some doctors, lawyers, carpenters, shopkeepers, and, yes, some capitalists and entrepreneurs. Greedy people exist in every walk of life, but it's bigotry to blame the whole group for the greed of some. One of the legitimate roles of government is policing harmful behavior, and the extent to which greedy members of any group succeed is a failure of government.

What identifies greed is its status as a capital sin. That is, if it leads to other bad behavior. If chasing money causes one to lie, cheat, or steal, it's greed. If looking for a quick buck leads you to try to use the government to help you at the expense of others, as in corrupted capitalism, then it's greed. Seeking legitimate sources of income and wealth is not greedy. Possessing substantial income or wealth, honestly obtained, is not the result of greed but excellent fiscal management.

SUMMARY: What Is Trade?

Trade is the basis of economic systems. Money only exists to make trade easier. Money only fills that role effectively when its value is held constant when compared to the value of goods and services being produced. The gold standard was one way to do this. Another would be to tie the money supply of a nation to that nation's gross domestic product. Most countries today use fiat money that the government controls the supply of artificially.

We live in an exciting time when it is easier than ever to create a business for ourselves. More and more people can forgo the security of working for a middleman for the riskier freedom of self-employment. This allows those who choose to do so a direct way to get a larger share of the rewards for value they create. However, those who choose the security of using a middleman—an employer—are not being exploited; they are trading some of the rewards for the work they are doing in exchange for the security of not having to risk going it alone.

People are not equal. No two people are equal. People must be equal in the eyes of the law and society, but trying to create a society where everyone has an equal life is both unfair and impossible. We are all unique, and that's wonderful. Our freedom to express our individuality will necessarily produce unequal outcomes, and that's wonderful too.

Evidentiary economics—examining the evidence for the success and failure of differing economic systems—proves that capitalism succeeds in providing a better life for the people than any other system. Socialism always fails because it is based on illogical philosophy rather than reality. As a result, it has failed every time it has been tried.

Capitalism works because it creates wealth that everyone shares. In a fixed economy, the only way to get more is to take from others, but in a capitalist, growth economy the way to getting more is to create more and share it.

We now live in an achieving society, where more than ever before in history we are able to reap the rewards of our efforts by creating value for others.

[6]

What Is Marx Madness?

Socialism is based on the theories of Karl Marx. Marx was insanely ignorant of economic principles in general and capitalism in particular. Marx began from the premise that capitalism exploits and oppresses the worker and claimed that companies and employers do the same. It's nonsense. As we've already discussed, companies and employers are middlemen that simply bring together the producers—the workers—and the consumers—the buying public. But there's more to it.

Oppression and exploitation require the use of force. No employer can force anyone to do anything. They may have rules and expectations they want their employees to adhere to, but the employees are free to go elsewhere.

Sorry to interrupt, but during the second industrial revolution, didn't people work in factories in terrible conditions without being able to leave because jobs were scarce?

Well, that's a great question, but to understand the answer, you'll have to put aside what you know about life today. The hundred years from 1820 to 1920 in the United States were the most tumultuous in history. Neither before nor since had so much about daily life changed in so short a time. In 1820, about 80 percent of the population lived and worked on farms.[1] A hundred years later, only 26 percent did so.[2] Farm life in the United States in 1820 was arduous; it was a life you were born into, and there was no hope of advancement or improvement of one's condition. There was little recreation or entertainment. It meant working ten, twelve, or more hours a day with no time off except church on Sunday and a church social once a month. Agrarian people were self-sufficient; they did everything for themselves. Occasionally, neighbors would help each other with daunting tasks like barn raising or harvesting.

As hard as it was, the conditions in Ireland were worse. Most Irish farmers lived on tiny subsistence farms; for many, potato was their primary food source. During the Great Famine in the late 1840s and early 1850s, about an eighth of Ireland's population starved, and about a fourth emigrated, most to the United States.[3] So a large part of the answer to your question is that as bad as the conditions were in the US cities during that time, most of those coming to the cities came from far worse lives. For them, it was a chance, a condition they saw as temporary, but with hope for improvement—and for most, it was.

The second part of the answer lies in what we economists call an externality, a noneconomic event that causes economic consequences. In this case, the externality was population growth. The US population grew from under nine million to over one hundred million during these hundred years.[4] The cities struggled as the population moved from farms here and abroad to cities. Millions poured into US cities from other parts of the country and the world. Your question refers to the apex of this period from about 1865 to 1885. During this time, the United States crossed the line between an agricultural nation and an urban manufacturing nation. During these twenty years, the population increased by more than 60 percent, most of which concentrated in the cities.[5] This growth challenged every aspect of life to adapt faster than ever before.

New housing couldn't keep up and was horribly overcrowded. Manufacturing struggled to keep up with the increased consumer demand, which led to factories being overcrowded and unable to modernize fast enough to improve working conditions. Trying to keep up meant long hours for workers in far less than ideal conditions while the glut of labor depressed wages. The cities were terribly polluted. In New York City, there were 150,000 horses in 1880, a horse for every six people. My two horses each produce about 30 pounds of manure daily and a couple of gallons of urine. That translates to 4,500,000 pounds of manure and 300,000 gallons of urine every day in New York City.[6] Imagine the streets of the cities. In addition, raw sewage was dumped into the rivers and lakes, polluting them. Belching smokestacks polluted the air to a degree never before imagined.

However, the people kept coming, mainly because, for most, it meant an improved quality of life. It meant a more reliable source of income, with housing that included flush toilets, running water, and better access to food. The cities and towns provided markets, schools, and improved health care. This improvement in quality of life was substantial. Figure 2 shows the path of that improvement. The solid line shows a crucial measurement many ignore: the labor-goods ratio. This ratio measures the quantity of goods a fixed amount of labor can purchase. Folks tend to overlook it when talking about inflation, but it is the only measurement that accurately describes the value of work in terms of goods. The chart shows that the Civil War had a devastating effect, but from 1870 to 1880, conditions improved somewhat, and from 1880 to 1890, they improved dramatically. So much so that by the end of the hundred years, an hour's labor could buy four times what it could

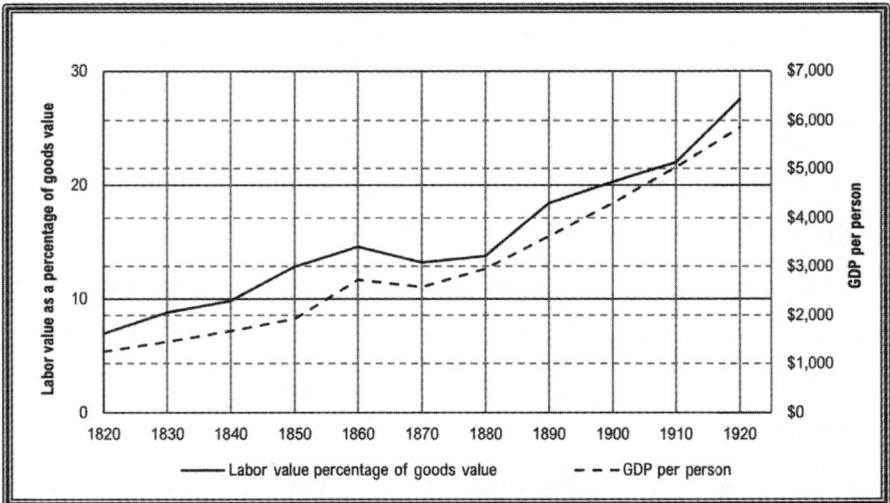

Figure 2. Growth in labor value and GDP per person

in 1820. We look back and see things from our current perspective where the labor-goods ratio is more than 100 percent, about four times what it was then.

The dashed line shows the gross domestic product per person, which is a good indicator of the standard of living. After the decline caused by the war, it is clear that from 1870 on, the standard of living increased dramatically. Over 1820 to 1920, it grew more than four and a half times.[7] This growth was unprecedented in human history. Never before and nowhere else had this magnitude of improvement in the human condition occurred.

Furthermore, it led to even more significant improvements to come. The US per capita GDP in 2024 was $86,600, fifteen times higher than in 1920.[8] This disparity warps our perception of a "normal" standard of living. What we would likely view as an intolerable life, those experiencing it saw it as an improvement and a chance for a better life. Also, life expectancy increased during these one hundred years from thirty-eight to fifty-four years[9]— another first in human history and a rate of improvement about the same as today.

When thinking of this period, many express concern about child labor, but it, too, is biased by a lack of understanding. Even as late as 1920, two-thirds of child labor was on farms rather than factories.[10] On the farm, children started work at five or six years old. Child labor was seen as beneficial, as it prepared children for the world of work and kept them from the temptation of idleness. Also, most agrarian families simply couldn't afford to raise a child without the compensation their labor afforded. In the cities, orphanages placed children in work situations to prepare them to lead productive lives.

Income in cities and towns exceeded that on the farm, and included benefits such as shops, saloons, festivals, libraries, sports, live music, plays, and museums. A further attraction was the increase in the size of the dating pool. Both genders found a far broader choice of available mates.

Unions have repeatedly boasted that they created the eight-hour day and the forty-hour workweek. The eight-hour day was first publicized by a Welsh manufacturer, Robert Owen, in 1817, who coined the phrase "eight hours labor, eight hours recreation, eight hours rest." The eight-hour day and the five-day, forty-hour workweek were "normalized" when Henry Ford instituted it for his employees in 1926.[11] He did it because it improved efficiency, so many other companies followed suit. Congress finally followed along in 1940. The people lead progress in a democratic society. The government always needs to catch up to the popular sentiment. Today's benefits are the legacy of increasing enlightenment in the population, not the result of unions or government. The people create unions, and the people elect the government, and business owners are people too, and many are more enlightened than the general population. Free people made life today better and will continue to improve life for tomorrow.

The companies were not oppressors; they were liberators. Only governments can be oppressive since only they have the power. Marx wanted to replace private employers with a single employer, the government—the only entity capable of exploitation and oppression.

Capitalism has no power; it has no means to exploit anyone. The idea of capitalism being exploitative was one part of Marx's exceptionally naive view of the world. It reflected a complete lack of understanding of economics. He needed to understand more of the things we have already discussed: value, labor, and trade.

An example of those misunderstandings is evident in a statement by the Colorado Education Association (CEA), the state affiliate of the National Education Association (NEA) and Colorado's largest teachers' union. The resolution was leaked to an online news outlet called *The Lion* on May 3, 2023, and subsequently picked up by Denver newspapers and the national media. The CEA passed a resolution condemning capitalism. It says, "CEA believes that capitalism requires exploitation of children, public schools, land, labor, and/or resources and, therefore, the only way to fully address systemic racism (the school to prison pipeline), climate change, patriarchy (gender and LGBTQ disparities), education inequality, and income inequality is to dismantle capitalism and replace it with a new, equitable economic system."[12]

This statement from the CEA expresses the socialist or Marxist view of capitalism. The CEA's condemnation of capitalism reveals a profound misunderstanding of capitalism and a startling lack of knowledge about the system's operation. This ignorance is shocking coming from educators, who we expect to be well-informed about the subjects they teach.

While this response to the statement addresses the CEA, it is a general response to Marxist and socialist indictments of capitalism. We discussed capitalism a little earlier, but now, let's address the errors and claims in the CEA statement starting with the misconception that capitalism necessitates exploitation. The statement is so erroneous that it is hard to know where to begin.

> **Unlike socialism, capitalism does not wield power over anyone or anything; therefore, it cannot exploit anyone.**

Let's be unequivocal: Capitalism does not exploit; it cannot exploit. It simply allows individuals willing to invest capital to create enterprises—middlemen—that provide a marketplace for producers—the workers—by catering to the needs and desires of others—the consumers. Unlike socialism, capitalism does not wield power over anyone or anything; therefore, it cannot exploit anyone. Exploitation and oppression necessitate the power to force or coerce others. Teachers, as government agents, possess that power; capitalism does not. This absence of power is a frequently misunderstood yet fundamental aspect of capitalism, and it is crucial to correct this misconception to foster trust in the system's integrity.

The CEA's statement begins by claiming that capitalism exploits children. Exploitation requires power, so who holds control over children? The only legitimate sources of authority are parents, teachers, the school system, and various governments.

There are also illegitimate forces like bullies and criminals. Today, if parents exploit children, they are subject to criminal charges. There are some limits on teachers exploiting children, but in most jurisdictions, there are no limits on exploitation by belief coercion. Belief coercion is a form of psychological manipulation that pressures individuals to act in ways contrary to their beliefs or values. More than thirty years as an educator has made it painfully clear to me that far too many teachers are guilty of this.

School systems are subject to even fewer restrictions than individual teachers. They are free to adopt belief-coercing curricula with little or no authority to mitigate their actions. School systems, as an arm of government, have the power to exploit anyone they elect to, including children. If the CEA is genuinely concerned about the exploitation of children, an investment in a mirror is warranted since CEA members are the most proximal source with the power to do so.

If capitalism cannot exploit children, it follows that capitalism also cannot exploit schools. Once again, exploitation requires power. Capitalism has no power or even influence over public schools. So, where does the power over public schools lie? The only entities that can exert control over public schools are governing boards, unions like the CEA, and various other parts of the government. The CEA is attempting to deny the power it holds and attribute the misuse of that power to capitalism, which has no control over schools. The CEA's pretense that it has no power is an example of how Marxists use the straw man of capitalist exploitation to create a society oppressed by socialism.

What is a straw man?

A straw man is a weak argument presented just for the purpose of defeating it. It stems from the idea of defeating an opponent "made of straw" who is weak and ineffectual. An example I see regularly is that "capitalists only care about making money." The writer then generally proceeds to prove that only caring about money is evil, therefore capitalists are evil. Of course, capitalists care about far more than money. For most, money is not even their primary concern. Another common example occurs when a policy difference is attacked by inference. "We need a $15 minimum wage to help people. Our opponents clearly don't care about people." The people who are opposed to a minimum wage are not doing so because of a lack of caring but because they see a more complex issue that harms more people than it helps. The straw man is a common propaganda technique based on distorting an argument and then attacking the distortion rather than the undistorted reasoning behind it.

Getting back to the CEA, doesn't capitalism control who owns property?

The CEA claims that capitalists control the land. I don't see how. Yet again, we must ask who has the power to control land: property owners, homeowner associations, and governments. Capitalism as a system has no control over land; however, capitalists may be property owners who can control the land they own within the limits prescribed by law. Zoning laws, environmental regulations, and other legal frameworks set the limits that govern land use and ownership. Since governments set those limits, those complaining should direct any exploitation complaints by property owners to the appropriate government body. If government fails to protect the people, the government is to blame, not the capitalists.

Does capitalism exploit labor?

If you've read this far, you already know that employers cannot exploit employees. In this context, though, the question is who holds the power over labor? Since the CEA is a union in a state without a right-to-work law, they have control over their workers. A right-to-work law is a statute that prohibits union security agreements, or agreements between labor unions and employers, that govern the extent to which an established union can require employees' membership, payment of union dues, or fees as a condition of employment, either before or after hiring. So, in a non-right-to-work state, the CEA can demand that workers join the union and pay dues. That sounds exploitative to me. In addition, since they are public employees, their members are not employed by private businesses of any kind and are unaffected by private capital investment. Therefore, only the union, the school district's governing board, and the relevant governments have the power to exploit labor. Capitalists are investors who cannot exert any control over laborers.

Does capitalism exploit resources?

This complaint by the CEA and socialists in general is meaningless, since it does not specify the resources or ownership. Everyone has power over some resources and no control over others. Businesses can control their resources, and the government can limit any control over any resource. As a system, capitalism has no control of any resource and, therefore, no means of exploitation. Of course, free-market capitalism allows companies to use resources to create products, but they do so in a manner prescribed by law. Again, if you don't like the laws, your dispute is with the government, not capitalism. Exploitation requires power; capitalism has none.

The second part of the statement in the CEA's resolution lists what they believe capitalism opposes addressing. However, they fail to understand that capitalism is an economic system with no mechanism for favoring or opposing anything. The Marxists in the CEA want some power to force society to ascribe to their vision of the ideal world. Capitalism does not have that power, so the CEA Marxists want to replace it with an oppressive socialist regime that does have that power.

However, individual capital investors—the capitalists— include most of the US population. How does this population feel about the issues CEA lists? Polling indicates pluralities question the existence of systemic racism, and those who do believe it exists believe that businesses are by far the institutions most likely to solve the problem and governments the least likely. A large majority of capitalists, including stockholders, favor taking steps to address climate change. The CEA also lists patriarchy as not solved by capitalism, but women are almost as invested in markets as men and perform better.

The CEA also listed educational inequality; that seems odd.

Yes, they also believe that capitalism does nothing to fix educational inequality. Still, the CEA represents the teachers, the most significant component of the system, and that would be primarily their responsibility. Furthermore, the disparity between White students and students of color in Denver Public Schools is substantial. The CEA's candidates have complete control of the local governing board. While 72 percent of White students score above grade level on the statewide literacy test, only 25.8 percent of Black and Hispanic students do so.[13] Also, White students are getting three times the education of students of color. Is that the educational equality they seek? And what does it have to do with capitalism?

As to income inequality, the CEA fails to recognize that income inequality is far worse in socialist countries like North Korea and Venezuela. According to the World Bank, the United States Gini income index, a measure of income inequality, was last calculated for most nations in 2020, and stood at 39.7, the lowest for the United States since 1992.[14] But, more importantly, the US index of 39.7 is very close to the world average of 37.8 and well within the average range. Read the biography of anyone who has lived in North Korea and knows from personal experience, and you will find that income inequality is far worse there than here. In Marxist socialist countries, the government officials and their pets have everything, and the people have nothing. That's part of why individuals risk their lives to get out. I don't see many people leaving the United States to escape income inequality, and I can't imagine anyone risking their lives to do so.

The core of capitalism is economic freedom and private property rights. Capitalism has rescued billions of people from poverty and raised living standards far beyond anything our ancestors imagined. The free market and true, uncorrupted capitalism are almost miraculous in that the spontaneous order created by the combination of individual choices that make up the free market can order an economy with no organized direction and do so in the best interests of the citizenry. This freedom underscores the power of individual choices in shaping the economy and society, making us all feel empowered and influential. No other economic system has ever provided greater good to more people. Capitalism's failures result from corruption, primarily a problem of government action to advantage some over others or government inaction to enforce a level, competitive marketplace.

Is capitalism successful for more than economic improvement?

Absolutely. It has significantly enhanced the quality of life, elevated living standards, and fostered economic freedom and prosperity. We should all appreciate and be grateful for these tangible benefits of capitalism. Capitalism, far from being an exploitative system, is a catalyst for prosperity and peace. Its benefits extend to children, public schools, land, labor, and resources, contrary to the claims of the CEA.

The stability it fosters is evident in the fact that capitalist nations do not engage in wars with each other. In fact, there has never been a conflict between two or more large, well-established free-market capitalist democracies. The only instances of war involve fascist-socialist dictatorships, which are known to wage war against both free-market democracies and each other. This stability and peace are the direct results of the economic freedom and private property rights that form the core of capitalism, providing a sense of security and reassurance.

Understanding all the weaknesses of socialism requires a relatively complete understanding of socialism as a system and the constraints it imposes. It also involves understanding two different worldviews. Whether you are religious or not, understanding the worldview of the world's major religions is essential. All these religions believe that humans do not always work and play well with others and, therefore, require religious and/or government control to keep the peace. Thus, these religions all have codes of conduct to achieve a peaceful society and support governments enforcing these, as well as a limited number of other codes and regulations. However, they acknowledge that governments are composed of humans who are as flawed as those they govern and, therefore, must require careful monitoring.

The socialist worldview holds that humans misbehave only because society—including religions and free-market capitalism—exploits them. They believe that if everyone experienced equal outcomes in the world, as outlined in John Lennon's song "Imagine," there would be world peace at all levels. Lennon imagines a world with no religions, countries, or possessions. But equal outcomes are inherently unequal.

Why do you say that?

Giving everyone the same things means many will get something they don't want or care about, and others will not get items that are important to them. Providing everyone with the same goods and services denies each person's unique humanity. Furthermore, when socialists take power, their flawed humanity has always come to the surface; the people are made poorer, and the elite rulers live in luxury.

There is absolutely no objective evidence to support their worldview. On the contrary, all the evidence reinforces the idea that humans will not work and play well with others without a means of regulating their behavior. Society is not the creator of individual misbehavior; society exists to mitigate it.

The socialist worldview leads to authoritarianism. It begins with the nationalization of the nation's industries and the seizure of private property. Once the government has taken over the means of production, it becomes responsible for creating and marketing all consumer goods. But this government takeover comes with a glaring flaw. According to US Small Business Administration estimates, almost one-third of new businesses fail in two years, half in the first five years, and two-thirds in the first ten.[15] If the government creates the enterprises, then most of their plans would also be expected to fail in ten years. Because of the high failure rate, the government tends to be cautious to a fault, bypassing many terrific ideas.

Capitalists are free to take more risks than the government because they risk their own money, not the people's. The willingness of capitalists to take significant risks has led to the creation of virtually all of the life-enhancing products we enjoy daily. We've learned that capitalists are not exploiting the people because exploitation requires power, which the capitalists don't have. Those who think otherwise get that backward; the people use the capitalists.

In a free market, many entrepreneurs try to develop products or services they think people want, but many fail. However, under government control, all the eggs are in one basket, so it's all or nothing. Capitalists fund entrepreneurs. They take a considerable risk when investing their money in new, unproven ventures. If the enterprise fails, the capitalists take all the loss, but the people take the loss when the government's plans fail.

Awhile ago, we discussed early trading. As civilization spread and population increased, people found they could produce more food more efficiently by farming. Farming required a new way of thinking; it meant investing resources, seeds, and labor for a profit—food in the future. This new way of thinking was the birth of capitalism, which is investing capital—your resources—for future gain. Capitalism is investing in the future. Capital is an accumulation, a store of accumulated assets minus accumulated liabilities. People tend to think of it monetarily, but that's an unnecessarily limiting view.

Assets add to your well-being, and liabilities reduce your well-being. In any area, monetary or otherwise, if you take your assets and subtract your liabilities, the result is your capital. Someone in good physical condition has more physical assets than liabilities. They have a store of physical capital. That capital allows them to fight off disease and disability more readily.

A capitalist is anyone who invests their capital in hopes of increasing their assets in the future. It is a commitment to the future. I call capitalism a commitment to hope. Capitalism, at its core, is about investing in the future, about believing that today's sacrifices will lead to tomorrow's rewards. For example, if someone in good physical condition tires themselves out today by exercising, temporarily depleting their physical capital in hopes of improving their physical condition, they are a capitalist. They are using assets they have today in hopes of receiving increased assets—a profit—in the future. Others may see the impact of this increased capital and be envious. They would also like to have those assets, but they haven't seen the capitalist's investment in building their capital and the risks the capitalist took.

Would education be another example of capitalism?

Yes, education can be another example of capitalism. One idea of education is investing time and other resources today, believing it will increase future ability, such as pursuing a college degree in a high-demand field like computer science. The second idea is to invest resources to learn more about something that interests you, whether or not it increases your future capability. Someone who studies art history purely out of personal interest, with no intention of using it professionally, would be an example of this view. Both are valid points of view but are often confused, with unfortunate consequences.

The first is the capitalist view, using capital today in hopes of increasing capital later. The second is using resources today for enjoyment. The difficulty arises when one chooses the second, expecting the rewards of the first. Pursuing a college degree in art history may be very rewarding today, but it may be something other than an asset in the future. Learning a skill is usually a capitalist undertaking. It is investing resources today for a reward in the future.

Playing a musical instrument well requires effort and dedication, which most consider more challenging than enjoyable. Still, it may lead to career opportunities or a future of enjoying the ability. Others invest in skills more clearly aimed in one direction or another. Welding is more likely to lead to career opportunities than result in a fun hobby. Still, knitting is less likely to lead to career opportunities and more likely to result in an enjoyable pastime in the future. Both are examples of capitalism because they are investments today for future rewards.

On the flip side, there's the anti-capitalist sentiment, often summarized as "Eat, drink, and be merry, for tomorrow you die." This perspective rejects the idea of risking today's rewards for potentially greater rewards in the future. It's a stance that can lead to future challenges and difficulties, a reality we must be aware of and prepared for. It only works really well if you actually die tomorrow.

Don't socialists say that capitalists are just fat cats who exploit the little guy?

That's a myth. Anyone who saves or invests money in a manner that creates capital is a capitalist. Capitalists include anyone who buys savings bonds, puts money in a savings account, invests in a retirement plan, or buys stocks. All these actions involve investing money to create a more significant amount for future use instead of spending it today. Furthermore, many more people are indirect capitalists. When someone buys insurance, they give money to the insurer who invests it in capital enterprises and uses some of the profits to pay claims.

Marxist anti-capitalists have spent the last 150 years using all the propaganda techniques available to convince people that capitalism is evil. They do this because capitalism means economic freedom, essential to civil liberty, and anti-capitalists fear freedom because it vanquishes their desire for power and control. They understand that significant undertakings require large amounts of capital. If private citizens cannot provide that capital, it must come from the government. If the government invests, then the government has control of it. In free-market capitalism, thousands or millions of shareholders share the power. The Marxist anti-capitalists don't want that because they believe they can more easily manipulate the government than millions of citizens. The anti-capitalist maxim I mentioned earlier of eating, drinking, and being merry because you'll die tomorrow works out well only if you actually die tomorrow. The socialist anti-capitalist takes the short-term view, believing it is better to spend resources for today's pleasure and worry about tomorrow, tomorrow. Whereas, the capitalist takes the long-term view, believing that a better future is worth investing resources in.

The capitalist uses resources to create more resources, while the anti-capitalist uses up resources today and hopes more will appear later. To be a capitalist is to adopt a way of life that invests in the future, not only with money but with health, education, training, relationships, reputation, and most other areas of life.

Furthermore, socialism always leads to tyranny. After taking control of the national economy, the government employs experts to plan every detail of the economy. Unfortunately, this expert planning has a fatal flaw: You cannot plan what you cannot predict. This is because human action continually undermines planning goals. No experts are omniscient enough to plan an economy. The problem is not that they are not smart enough but that the task is beyond human capability. Their error is in not recognizing that fact.

The "experts" create a five-year plan but find the people frequently prefer something other than what they decide the people should have. Some people don't work as hard as the plan calls for. Those in charge often find that changing conditions mean their plans don't work out. To solve these problems, the government takes greater control of people's lives. They decide who does what job, who lives in what house, and what goods everyone receives. Of course, people don't like that. Life without choice isn't paradise; it's hell!

At least, that's what all the evidence shows. This extraordinary control leads to a discontent citizenry who would vote for something else if given a chance. When the government sees the writing on the wall, meaningful elections disappear. Opponents disappear or have fatal "accidents," and dissidents quickly learn that opposition is not tolerated. Those running the government are committed to socialism and will not allow an election that threatens to replace it. Instead, the people may get to vote for a choice between candidates who are both pledged to continue the current system but not to retrieve their freedom.

This attempt to control the citizenry is not only inhumane; it can never work. Since government officials are the only ones creating products, there are no competing products. This economic hegemony means there is only one product for every need. One model of car, one kind of telephone, one kind of computer, one kind of bread; there is no consumer choice of product, only government choice. This lack of choice almost always leads to a black market, an underground free market that attempts to get what the people want to the people. However, if these violators are caught, they are locked up or killed.

Why do socialist countries persecute religious groups?

Since the world's major religions place a supreme being as one's first loyalty, socialist governments either outlaw or suppress religion so the head of government, the supreme leader, becomes the citizenry's first loyalty. The socialists replace the people's religions with the socialist religion. However, these repressions of the populace fail to solve the problem, so the government imposes still stricter controls on the people.

When people object to these oppressions, they are imprisoned or killed. Socialist governments have killed over a hundred million people in their attempts to stifle dissent and incarcerated millions more.[16] People begin to flee the country to areas of greater freedom. This results in rigid border restrictions. This difference in border security may be the most severe indictment of socialist regimes.

> **Countries with free-market capitalism police their borders to prevent unauthorized entry, but socialist countries police their borders to prevent citizens from escaping.**

Countries with free-market capitalism police their borders to prevent unauthorized entry, but socialist countries police their borders to prevent citizens from escaping. As a result, people risk their lives to get into capitalist countries or get out of socialist countries. The progression of increasing government control under socialism is unavoidable. Economic control must always lead to total control because economic freedom is critical to personal liberty. There can be no individual freedom once economic freedom is lost.

In 2023, 24,000 Chinese asylum seekers crossed the border from Mexico to the United States, which was up more than ten times compared to the year before.[17] They said they sought to escape an increasingly repressive political climate and bleak economic prospects. The United Nations has projected that China will lose 310,000 people through emigration in 2024. In addition, China was expected to lose more millionaires in 2024 because of migration than any other country. So many wealthy Chinese are trying to get their kids out of the country by sending them to foreign schools that the growth in foreign schools is booming, most notably the little-known Singapore International School of Bangkok. It is Thailand's only exchange-listed school operator, and the Chinese student influx has made the school one of the best stock investments in the world and its chief executive officer a multimillionaire.

Early in our discussions, you mentioned you practice evidentiary economics. Can you say more about that and how it applies to economic systems?

As you know, economics is the study of how we choose to allocate our resources. Every living creature must make economic decisions. Fundamentally, the goal is survival. If an organism burns more calories looking for food than it gains in calories from the food it finds, it dies. Economics is a quest for the most efficient use of resources. Evidentiary economics approaches this problem by seeking evidence of what works best. While that may seem obvious, many so-called economic discussions revolve around what some wish the most efficient practices were rather than examining the evidence to substantiate their beliefs. Evidentiary economics examines the evidence to discover methods that maximize benefit and minimize cost. This approach applies to individual, local, and national choices.

Evidentiary economics differs from philosophical economics. Earlier, I mentioned the John Lennon song "Imagine." Its lyrics best characterize philosophical economics. Lennon, as talented as he was, needed an economics education. The song's title explains his point of view; he imagines a world that does not exist. Is Lennon's imaginary world better than this one? Who knows, but proposed economic solutions designed for a mythical world cannot help us more efficiently use resources in the real world.

Evidentiary economics begins with the premise that human beings, like all organisms, are motivated to a great extent by self-interest. Of course, it's okay to "imagine" that we were otherwise and dream Utopian dreams, but people are people, and thousands of years of human history support this view. That doesn't mean people are naturally evil, but the evidence tells us that sometimes self-interest escalates into greed, and then people are capable of terrible deeds.

We discussed Plato earlier, and I mentioned that his pupil Aristotle pointed out that Plato's collectivist ideas failed on logical grounds. Aristotle responded that the group can only exist with individuals who are different. They have different needs and desires, and a philosopher-king could never please them all, no matter how well-motivated. Unfortunately, that hasn't stopped socialists from trying and repeatedly failing to find a way to create a mythical Utopia.

You keep saying socialism always fails. Where's the evidence of these failures?

Earlier, we discussed the failures of the *Mayflower* experiment. That wasn't the only time America tried socialism to have it fail. In 1607, the first English settlers in America created a colony about one hundred miles south of present-day Washington, DC. They called their settlement Jamestown. The colonists began their community as a socialist endeavor. They required all the members to relinquish all assets produced to "the common store." There was no buying or selling and no trade except with Indigenous people. And there was no private property.

The lack of private property creates a situation where it is not in the individual's self-interest to work hard. Author John Cooke writes in his book *Virginia: A History of the People*, "It was a premium for idleness, and just suited the drones, who . . . promptly decided that it was unnecessary to work themselves, since others would work for them."[18]

Before long, this socialist enterprise created disaster. At a time and place where requiring every individual's utmost effort was necessary to prevent collapse, the lack of perceived rewards led to the "starving time." The colony suffered more than one hundred casualties, and those who were there reported that people resorted to eating pets and shoe leather. George Percy, the colony's temporary leader while John Smith was in England, said, "And now famine beginning to look ghastly and pale in every face that nothing was spared to maintain life and to do those things which seem incredible, as to dig up dead corpses out of graves and to eat them, and some have licked up the blood which hath fallen from their weak fellows."[19]

How can trying to do good turn out so badly?

Because they based their ideas on how to do good on a fantasy that ignored the real world. After Smith returned from England, he tried everything he could think of to make socialism work, including threats to withhold food from those who did not work. Nothing helped, and the economy continued to struggle.

How did they fix it?

In 1611, the new governor, Thomas Dale, began reversing the communal store system. He persuaded the London Company to grant a fifty-acre plot to any colonist willing to clear and farm it. This shift to a free-market economy, where every individual's self-interest was aligned with hard work, led to a significant improvement. Colonist John Rolfe, the man who married Pocahontas (not John Smith, as the legend claims), said that after abolishing the common stores system and restoring private property, the colonists began gathering and reaping the fruits of their labors with "much joy and comfort." According to history writer M. P. Andrews in *Virginia: The Old Dominion*, "As soon as the settlers were thrown upon their own resources, and each freeman had acquired the right of owning property, the colonists quickly developed what became the distinguishing characteristic of Americans—an aptitude for all kinds of craftsmanship coupled with an innate genius for experimentation and invention."[20]

Did the *Mayflower* colony also reintroduce private property?

Yes. In 1763, Bradford, like Governor Dale in Jamestown, consigned to all healthy persons or families their own plots of land. The introduction of private property led to an immediate change in the colonists' behavior. Almost overnight, a body of industrious, hard-working producers replaced feigned illness and idleness. Men, women, and even children eagerly went to their fields and labored tirelessly to improve their lives. This new, private property, free-market economy changed life in the colony from an unpleasant, unsuccessful endeavor into a dynamic community resulting in a bountiful harvest, and they held a thanksgiving celebration to rejoice in their success.

Trying to build a better world is something we can all aspire to, and we can, but not with socialism. Socialism could only work if human beings were saints, but all of the world's major religions remind us they are not. We recognize saintly or astonishingly good individuals because they are so rare.

If you want to see the difference between shared ownership and private property, you only need to take a drive. As you cruise along the roadway, you'll see litter. If you go down an empty dirt road, you will probably encounter "wildcat dumps," where folks who don't want to go all the way to a public dump site, dump what they wish. And notice the road signs shot full of holes.

Now, contrast that with the private property you encounter. Driveways and front yards are usually not littered with discarded soda cups, paper trash, and beer bottles. They don't have dumped refrigerators and old couches lying around. The signage in the yard usually doesn't have bullet holes.

The difference between public and private property illustrates what is generally called the tragedy of the commons. This tragedy occurs because people have insufficient motivation to expend effort that doesn't benefit them. We may wish it were otherwise, as socialists do, but it is in our DNA and that of all other living things to pursue our own self-interest. Lennon may have imagined otherwise, but the system he imagined never works.

How come we haven't been taught this?

Ideology blinds many economists, so they can't see what the evidence shows them. Furthermore, as I said earlier, the Marxist anti-capitalists have spent the last 150 years using all the propaganda techniques available to convince people that capitalism is evil. They fear it and hate it. The fact you are just learning this proves the point.

Anti-capitalists exert a considerable measure of control over education, as we discussed earlier in talking about the manifesto of the Colorado Education Association. However, the anti-capitalist view is wrong; evidence does not support it. Capitalism happens naturally, whereas socialism is based on force. Evidentiary economics assumes that economic decisions must depend on how people behave rather than how we wish they would. Economic systems must allow human self-interest to advance the common good by allowing competition to get the best from everyone. Whether we like it or not, it's human nature.

That sounds pretty selfish to me.

Selfishness and self-interest are different, as you may recall from our earlier discussions. Selfishness is self-interest run amok. Private property and free-market capitalism harness this self-interest into spontaneous order. Free markets take the desire to make a better life and use it to build a trading economy that benefits everyone.

Socialism believes it can magically convert all humans into saints despite thousands of years of experience teaching us otherwise. Because of this erroneous assumption, socialism always fails. It has never made a better life for anyone except for the ruling elite in countries that impose it; these rulers get rich on the backs of the poor. In free-market capitalism, those who get rich do so by marketing products and services that benefit everyone.

Have you spent much time with small children? Two-year-olds take each other's toys, hurt, and tease each other. They do this and have done this in every culture and every economic construct throughout human history. When children take each other's toys, it's not because they are societally deprived. They simply want what someone else has, often irrespective of how much they already have. All the world's major religions are concerned with regulating human behavior. It is a universal acknowledgment that people have some tendency to harm others.

But don't capitalists harm others by taking wealth for themselves at the expense of others?

No. The answer to your question lies in the difference between fixed and growth economies. Consider very early humans. Back then, innovation was minimal and slow to arrive. If you were living in a cave, you couldn't go out and build a new one, and the food supply was whatever was available in the environment; people didn't know about making more; the economy, such as it was, was fixed. It stayed the same; it was what it was. In this fixed kind of economy, the only way anyone could have more for themselves would be to take more of the fixed total, leaving less for others. It also had the effect of wiring the human race for scarcity.

In a fixed economy, the way to survive was to take what you could because there was only so much, and you had to fight for what you needed. However, we are still emotionally living in that past even though we no longer live in a world of scarcity but a world of abundance that is growing wealthier every day. Taking from others is no longer necessary to get what you need. Back then, the size of the pie was fixed. Everyone had to share the existing resources. Now, we bake a bigger pie. When resources are relatively fixed, that's what I mean by a pie of a specific size.

Over time, people began to trade and create innovation, but it still took a long time for innovations to happen because there was no accompanying reward for coming up with one. As I mentioned earlier, whoever invented the wheel may have put a lot of people out of work, but he probably didn't get rich. There was no patent office and no way to keep others from building their own wheels by simply copying the design. Some think that's how it should be.

Why should some get to have good stuff and not others?

Because if there are no rewards, people will not invest the time to create innovations, so they come along very rarely. How much did life on earth change in the two thousand years from 500 BC to 1500 AD? For most people, two thousand years of stagnation hardly changed at all. What changed after that? Freedom and free markets: From 1500 to 1800, free-market capitalism developed, beginning a growth economy. In this new growth economy, private investment began to spur economic growth. By economic growth, we mean not struggling to get a part of the existing wealth in the world, a fixed amount, but creating new wealth as a result of innovation.

In 1474, the Venetian Act codified the patenting process and created a system for applying for patents. Europe had the concept of patents. Officials punished people for theft of what we now call intellectual property. However, it was a haphazard process with no set standards. The Venetian Act required that the patent be for a unique and useful product. This patent revolution is when patents first became an incentive to innovate.

This birth of capitalism helped trigger the Renaissance, the rise of creativity in art and science that paved the way for what was to come. Over the next two or three hundred years, capitalism slowly grew. Then came the industrial revolution. It had some beginnings in Europe in the early 1700s. The first significant innovation to change the world was the atmospheric engine invented by Thomas Newcomen, which was the first commercially successful steam engine. It used a piston and cylinder, not unlike an automobile engine today. Newcomen invented it to pump water out of coal mines. This invention led to James Watt, a Scotsman, introducing a far more efficient design in 1765. Now, capitalism has entered the picture. Watt needed funds for advanced equipment and expensive parts to make further improvements. He partnered with venture capitalists to provide the funds for a share of the profits. In 1774, Watt was satisfied that he had sufficiently improved the design to begin marketing it. Watt's success led others to invent different and better engines. Indeed, venture capitalism played a pivotal role in igniting the industrial revolution. It provided the necessary funds for innovation, thereby accelerating progress and shaping the modern world.

So capitalists started the industrial revolution?

It's fair to conclude that. But then came the amplifier from across the Atlantic. America's founders were creating a new country and a new kind of government that encouraged innovation. The United States Constitution Article I, Section 8, Clause 8 states that Congress shall have power to "Promote the Progress of Science and useful Arts, by securing for limited Times to Authors and Inventors the exclusive Right to their respective Writings and Discoveries."

Three years later, the United States had a patent office and issued its first patent to Samuel Hopkins on July 31, 1790. This patent process triggered the most explosive burst of human progress ever seen. On June 19, 2018, the United States issued its ten millionth patent. For the first time in human history, life improved, first in the United States and then worldwide; each decade that passed resulted in more improvement than in all of recorded history until then.

Furthermore, innovation is accelerating. It took 120 years for the first million patents to be approved. Getting to two million took only twenty-four years. It took twenty-six years to get to three million, and thirteen years later, there were another million. Then fifteen years for the next million, then eight years, then seven years, then six years, then four years, and the ten millionth patent came only three years after the nine millionth. The first million took 120 years; at the current pace, the subsequent 120 years, ending in 2030, will likely see fourteen million patents in the same amount of time.[21] Innovation coming fourteen times faster means life will likely be fourteen times better. Free-market capitalism is driving this success. Life in 1500 was similar to two thousand years earlier for most people. Now, life is fourteen times better than it was 120 years ago.

Let's get back to the difference between fixed and growth economies. The difference is in what has changed in the last six hundred years, particularly the last two hundred years. Before 1500, virtually the entire world was a fixed economy. Trade improved conditions somewhat, but only a little for regular folk. When kings and queens and other royals acquired wealth, it was at the expense of everyone else. Hence, the legend of Robin Hood. Back then, the rich were exploiters, but now, the rich are primarily self-made innovators who boost the economy for everyone.

Another good way to measure the difference is GDP per capita per year. That is, how many goods and services the average person on Earth was able to create. That is, how much value could each person create to be shared by all? Until about 1700, it was less than $100 in today's dollars. By 1800, it was closer to $250. For the first time in human history, the pie's size and the world's collective wealth had more than doubled. By 1900, it had surpassed $1,000. By 1950, it was over $3,000. By 2000, the value each person created was approaching $7,000. By 2020, it was over $12,000. In 2024, it was $13,900 and is projected to be $14,450 in 2025.[22]

In the last three centuries, the size of the pie as measured by GDP per person has increased to 130 times its size for the previous two thousand years. Free-market capitalism funded innovation that increased per-person wealth by an astounding amount. In a fixed economy, the pie only grows in proportion to the population. In a growth economy, the pie grows in proportion to dollars invested in innovation.

It's astounding that a large part of Marx's hatred of capitalism was because he hated the changes that the progress generated by capitalism caused. He devoted about five pages of *The Communist*

Manifesto—almost 20 percent of it—to how the changes caused by progress hurt the working man. So his design of socialism was, in part, an attempt to create a system that would hamper progress. Marx admits that progress flourishes more under capitalism than socialism, and he thinks that's not a good thing. Why would anyone in today's world want to adopt a system that by today's standards is designed to fail? Socialism's failure is built in. It's not a bug; it's a feature.

Couldn't the government do the investing?

The US federal government owns 1.2 percent of the patents issued in the last fifty years. (Exact numbers before that are difficult to obtain, since the patents are granted by agency rather than a combined total. The best estimates are that before fifty years ago, the percentage was far lower, but to be safe, we will consider the higher number of 1.2 percent.) That means if we relied on the government, we would have 1/85 the innovation. The GDP per capita has increased 130 times in the last three hundred years, and 1/85 of 130 is 1.5. So, if we had left it to the government, the growth would have been 1.5 times more innovative and wealthy, compared to 130 times as much. In addition, venture capitalism is a risky business. Investors may lose $200 billion in a single year. When they do, no one is hurt but themselves.

If the government were doing it, that $200 billion would have to be paid by the taxpayers, requiring a 5 percent tax increase for that one loss. Many losses by many investors occur in the same year, meaning the tax increase could be ten times higher than that. About 90 percent of start-up businesses fail, and the investors lose their money. Do you want the government making bets like that with your money?

With their courage and significant financial risks, venture capitalists are our economy's unsung heroes. Many have lost fortunes, and many have made them back again and more. They sometimes get huge rewards for taking those risks, but those risks they take power the economy for all of us. They deserve a big reward because they are not taking an undeserved piece of a fixed pie. They are taking a smaller percentage of a pie by increasing its size.

Let's say the current pie size is $100. Now, entrepreneur Smith creates a product that increases productivity by 10 percent; Smith makes a profit of $5; in a pie of $100, that's huge, but Smith increased the pie to $110 by increasing productivity, so $5 is left for everyone else. This example is not a case of someone losing for someone else to win. No one lost; everyone is 5 percent richer. Who cares how much Smith made if we all get 5 percent richer? A growth economy is Robin Hood reimagined, not robbing from the rich to give to the poor but riding the coattails of the wealthy entrepreneurs to provide more to everyone. When I said we were wired for scarcity, I meant that negative feelings about the rich are holdovers from when the pie was a fixed size and the economy was a zero-sum game.

The more each of us creates for ourselves, the more we create for others. It's long past time to stop thinking of the rich as fat cat exploiters and appreciate their contributions. Not just to be nice but because understanding their endeavors as a necessary part of a positive-sum game is in our long-term self-interest. We should recognize the growth economy, the positive-sum game, for what it is: not just better for us but better for all humanity. The more each of us creates for ourselves, the more we create for others. We've replaced stealing and raiding with free-market trading so everyone can benefit.

SUMMARY: What Is Marx Madness?

Marx had a naive view of the world. We used the Marxist statement about capitalism as a means of refuting Marxist dogma line by line. Capitalism has no power. It cannot exploit, coerce, or harm anyone. Only a government, a king, a dictator, or a totalitarian socialist government like Marx imagines has the power to exploit. The power Marxists attribute to capitalism is imaginary. The power of capitalism lies with the consumer.

Marx madness is the deluded belief that an oppressive dictatorship is better for the people than capitalism. We've discussed how exploitation and oppression require force to compel behavior. Only government has that force. Marxist Socialism wishes to replace capitalism, which has no means to force anyone to do anything, with an all-encompassing government that can control every aspect of life.

The CEA's resolution is an excellent example of the ignorance and insanity of the Marxist position. The things they claim to be horrors of capitalism are imagined. Capitalism does not have the power to harm. Much of the exploitation they allege is perpetrated by their union and their cronies in government.

Capitalism is nothing more than investing for the future. Even squirrels are smart enough to employ capitalism by storing food for the future. The socialist fantasy means economic collapse. Capitalism works better than any system ever designed, and that's based on evidence not imagination.

Whereas socialism dreams of controlling every aspect of human life and replacing religion and culture with socialist doctrine, this can only be accomplished by oppressive tyranny. Marx Madness fails to recognize that in the modern world we enjoy a growth economy that does not require dividing fixed, limited assets. Capitalism generates wealth for all by creating more and better assets, which is a world of abundance not scarcity. Marx decries this economic growth, believing it is too disruptive for the masses to adjust to. Marx Madness wants to slow or stop progress. Marxism's repeated failures are not a bug; they are a feature.

[7]

What Is Crony Capitalism?

The term *capitalism* is often misused and misunderstood, leading to unwarranted negative perceptions. However, a correct understanding of free-market capitalism can alter those perceptions and provide individuals and policymakers with the knowledge to make informed decisions. This understanding will also reveal that much of the negative perception of capitalism stems from attributing government failure to market failure.

One example that serves particularly well is health care in the United States. In 1900, the average American spent about $100 per year in today's dollars on health care. As the quality of medicine increased, the costs rose to about 5 percent of annual income.[1] Hospitals had a problem maintaining a steady income during the Great Depression, which itself was a government failure. In 1930, Baylor University Hospital offered a deal to 1,250 Dallas public school teachers. The terms of this deal were that the teachers would each pay fifty cents a month and, in return, would get up to twenty-one days of hospital care at no additional charge. For a while, everything was fine; this system did not interfere with the free market.

However, this plan quickly caught on with other hospitals and eventually became Blue Cross. This system became readily available but not widely used until the government intervened in the economy, imposing wage and price controls during World War II. These wage and price controls created a labor shortage and resulted in the inability of firms to increase pay to attract workers, so they began to offer health insurance based on the Blue Cross model. In 1943, the IRS, in another government intervention, determined that these benefits should be tax-free and, in 1954, increased the benefit further. By 1960, most firms offered health-care benefits, and in constant dollars, between 1960 and 2015, medical professional incomes rose 300 percent. During the same period, the median income for all workers rose by less than one-tenth that much.[2] This inflationary behavior was entirely predictable since separating the consumer and producer prevents the consumer from shopping for the best deal, so prices rise. Because of the government intervention, medical insurance is unlike car or home insurance. In car and home insurance the consumer has a choice of dozens of competing companies to choose from, but in health insurance, competition is either limited or completely eliminated. There is apparent competition in health care, but it is a medical monopoly.

But monopolies can't exist without government allowance. Free-market capitalism relies on competition to regulate prices and increase productivity. Therefore, one of the crucial responsibilities of the government is to guarantee competitiveness by actively preventing monopolistic trade practices. Unfortunately, the government has been derelict in its duty in this regard. For example, only two corporations control 90 percent of Americans' beer.[3] Five banks control about half of the nation's banking assets. Many states have health insurance markets where the top two insurers have an 80–90 percent market share. In Alabama, one company, Blue Cross Blue Shield, has an 84 percent market share, and in Hawaii, it has a 65 percent market share.[4]

Regarding high-speed internet access, almost all markets are local monopolies; over 75 percent of households have no choice, with only one provider. Four players control the US beef market and have carved up the country. After two recent mergers, three companies will control 70 percent of the world's pesticide market and 80 percent of the US corn-seed market.[5]

Regulating monopolistic practices is one of the legitimate roles of government intervention in the economy, and the government has been unduly lax in doing so. This inaction has led to the concentration of power in the hands of a few, which stifles competition and innovation. Blaming "greedy capitalists" is not the correct way to think of it. Imagine instead someone is burglarizing your home, and you call the police, and the police offer to help— wait for it—the burglar. They give him a hand loading his car with your stuff. Of course, you're mad at the burglar, but I'll bet you'd be even more mad with the police.

The laissez-faire attitude of government officials toward regulating monopolistic practices is pretty similar to the burglar example.

The world has bad actors, including some capitalists. The reason we have government is to stop them, but too often, the government either stands by watching, doing nothing, or actively helping "the bad guys." Government does this in several ways including: bailouts, loan guarantees, monopoly advantage, no-bid contracts, occupational licensing, regulatory capture, subsidies or "corporate welfare," tariffs, tax privileges, and laws benefiting particular industries.

We'll cover several of these, but to begin let's use an example of laws benefiting particular industries. Arizona is an open range state. While no single law defines the open range, nine statutes on the books pertain to livestock and fences. Outside most urban areas, the property owner is responsible for fencing out livestock with a "lawful fence," with posts no farther than thirty feet apart and at least four strands of barbed wire spaced eighteen, twenty-eight, thirty-eight, and fifty inches above the ground. The problem is that unless you have such a fence and the livestock break through it or the livestock owner willfully herds his cattle onto your property, then you are responsible for damage done by the livestock. Furthermore, without a lawful fence, if the landowner harms or harasses the livestock or allows their dog to do so, the owner is liable for any damage to the trespassing livestock and can be charged with a misdemeanor. These laws apply on private property and anywhere on open range, including public roads. Therefore, if a driver strikes and kills livestock on a public road and is killed in the collision, the driver's heirs will be held liable for the cost of the livestock killed.

How do I know all this? I live in rural Arizona. I have about

140 acres. For you city folk, 140 acres is about twenty-two city blocks. I have spent hundreds of hours and thousands of dollars building and maintaining fences on my property to keep cattle out. I learned the hard way that if cattle get through a fence that does not meet the definition of a lawful fence, cattle can do hundreds of dollars in damage in a single day, and the owner of the cattle will not be held liable.

If a dog bites you, the owner of the dog is liable, but if a cow crashes through your patio door and eats your furniture, you're out of luck. The Arizona government implemented these laws to save ranchers the expense of fencing their land to keep their livestock contained, but they unfairly transferred the fencing burden to rural landowners. This is an example of laws benefiting particular industries to the detriment of the public.

These actions and inactions on the part of our government undermine the principles of free-market capitalism and threaten our economic system because they cause socialism to appear an attractive alternative by making it seem the capitalists are evil. In the preceding example, I don't blame the cattlemen for trying to save a buck, I blame the state of Arizona for passing laws to help them do it at my expense.

I've read that a "corporate veil" protects businesses from the consequences of their actions. Why is that?

The difficulty in piercing the corporate veil is a fundamental problem. The problem was serious fifty-five years ago, when the

Yale Law Journal reported, "Shareholders of real estate, entertainment, shipping, and manufacturing enterprises, for example, have successfully used limited liability to escape personal responsibility for the torts of their corporations. As a consequence, plaintiff law firms in metropolitan areas will often have two to three cases a year in which their client's recovery is thwarted by the corporate fiction."[6]

In the ensuing half century, the problem has only gotten worse. Common sense and common law indicate that everyone should be accountable for their actions and not be able to resort to legal loopholes to avoid responsibility. Again, this is a failure of the government. The government created the rules for corporation liability, and, of course, some bad actors will try to game the system to make illicit gains. The government needs to step up and change the rules to make this impossible or, at least, much more difficult.

I'm not saying that capitalists are "bad actors." I'm saying some people in every social context will try to manipulate and exploit societal rules to give them an advantage over others. Yes, some of them are capitalists, but the vast majority are not. Blaming all of them for the actions of a few is bigotry. Capitalism has had its failures, but the cause of most failures is corrupted capitalism, often called cronyism or crony capitalism.

This corruption of capitalism occurs when the government acts to advantage some actors over others. Many economists cite three components shaping cronyism: the basic microeconomic foundation of rent-seeking, the institutional-structural component of the embedding environment in which rent-seeking happens, and the ideological component providing legitimacy to the associated structures and processes.

Rent-seeking is a term economists use to refer to the attempt to gain undeserved profit. Profit is the reward capitalists and entrepreneurs receive for creating products and services that benefit society. Profit obtained by fraud or manipulation harms the economy, and it is up to the government to prevent and punish it.

Why isn't it punished?

Fraud cases are filed every day in this country, but preventing all forms of fraud is challenging because it is often cleverly disguised, and the government grants privileges to businesses, providing them an unfair advantage. Some examples of these privileges are bailouts, loan guarantees, monopoly advantage, no-bid contracts, occupational licensing, certificates of need, regulatory capture, subsidies, tariffs, and other measures to restrict foreign competition and tax privileges granted to foreign companies. Interest groups are responsible for enticing the government to provide this unfair advantage through lobbying, which is harmful to the economic welfare of society.

The power of lobbyists is an argument against capitalism often espoused by socialists, and in this case, they are right. I've never said that everything socialists believe is wrong. They see many of the same problems as we all do but misunderstand the issues and have the wrong solutions.

Lobbyists facilitate rent-seeking, which involves individuals or groups working on obtaining government financial transfers instead of contributing productive work that benefits society. Furthermore, lobbyists frequently lobby for government policies that benefit their clients but are an inefficient use of government resources. You've probably heard the stories of $640 toilet seats, $660 ashtrays, $436 hammers, $7,600 coffeemakers, and $74,000 ladders.[7]

There's much more. Another form of corrupted capitalism is occupational licensing. Twenty-one states have policies preventing the renewal of licenses if the one seeking the license has student loans in arrears. These laws are among the most subtle and damaging to the economically vulnerable. Occupational licensing is a form of government regulation requiring a license to pursue a profession or vocation for compensation.

While some forms of occupational licensing may be necessary to protect public safety, most are not. For example, requiring surgeons to receive some medical certification may be helpful. However, occupational licensing is often merely a way for established businesses or industries to use the power of the government to reduce competition. It is also one of the fastest areas of growth for corrupted capitalism. In the 1950s, only one in twenty US workers needed government permission to pursue their chosen occupation. Today, it is closer to one in three. Research has shown that licensing neither protects public health and safety nor improves products and services. However, it is highly effective in limiting the number of people who can create a job for themselves and earn a livable wage.

And there's more. Most states have "certificate of need" (CON) laws or "certificate of public convenience and necessity" (CPCN) laws. These laws are a type of licensing requirement that prevent many new businesses from starting. Unlike other licensing laws, CONs and CPCNs do not require education or training qualifications to obtain a business license. Instead, CONs and CPCNs only allow new businesses to open if they can show the state that new competition is in the public interest or necessary or needed. These laws are often called "competitor's veto laws." Existing businesses routinely use these laws to restrict the entry of competing companies into the industry. This misuse of the government is a corruption of capitalism by the government. It is not a failure of the free market.

Do you have any specific examples?

Sure, take, for example, the case of Kine Gueye. Kine grew up in a village in Senegal where every girl learns traditional African hair braiding. She moved to the United States and settled in Louisville, Kentucky. She sometimes worked twelve hours a day braiding hair in her Louisville home, earning between $80 and $250 per customer. As her practice expanded, so did her family. She married, had children, and moved her practice into a storefront. When she began advertising her services, the government shut down Kine because she did not have a cosmetology license. Getting such a license would require nearly two years of school and $16,000 in tuition. She had the necessary skills, and her work posed no threat to public safety. She fought back, and eventually, Governor Matt Bevin signed a bill in 2016 exempting hair braiders from the state's cosmetology regulations.[8] Nevertheless, a cronyist policy had attempted to prevent her from earning a living. Since the bill only exempts braiders, other budding entrepreneurs will have to fight for their own exemptions. This results in consumers getting fewer choices and higher prices.

There are hundreds more examples. Laws change every day, but according to the Institute for Justice, these were all in force in 2023. In Louisiana, florists must be licensed, and it costs almost $1,500 and over two thousand days to become licensed as an interior designer. Does the public need to be protected from rogue florists and interior designers? The state of Washington requires over $300 and more than 1,600 hours of classes to practice cosmetology. The other Washington—DC—requires over $700 to register as an auctioneer. It also requires a college degree to provide child day care.

Kansas makes funeral attendants pay $200 for a license. Maine makes would-be travel guides pay hundreds in fees and requires rigorous training and written and oral examinations to be paid to organize a camping trip. If you fall behind in paying your taxes in Maryland, the state automatically prohibits you from obtaining or renewing an occupational license.

So, in Maryland, if you don't have the money to pay your taxes, you lose the right to earn money to pay them. In one case, a dentist behind in his taxes was not allowed his dental license. The state court upheld the unpaid taxes law on the grounds that failing to pay taxes promptly made one unfit to practice dentistry. Maryland also requires a license to work as a physical trainer, a barber, a chauffeur, a manicurist, an upholsterer, or a taxidermist, among many others.

One of my friends is a massage therapist, and whenever she moves, she has to get a new license in the new state she practices in. In Virginia she even got a minister's license so she could put food on the table while waiting for the state to permit her to practice massage—even though she had double the required hours for that state.

Massachusetts requires a license for fortune tellers, presumably to protect the public from inaccurate predictions. Thirty-seven states require a license to shampoo hair without an average of eight months of training and apprenticeship. Until recent years, Arizona required six months of training for a special license to blow-dry hair—no cutting or dying, just blow-drying. In New York, where cosmetology requirements are lowest, a stylist needs half a year of training. Most states require more.

Tennessee requires barbers to have a high school diploma. Presumably because algebra and English literature are essential prerequisites for cutting hair. Michigan requires a license or qualifications to work as an airport manager, an animal control officer, an auto mechanic, a butter grader, a potato dealer, a finishing contractor, a forester, a court reporter, a landscape architect, a librarian, a painter, a plant grower, a property manager, a rain gutter installer, a roofer, or a siding installer.

And on and on it goes.

How did this corruption come about?

It's a long story, so bear with me. Crony capitalism or corrupted capitalism results from the government offering favors or advantages to some groups at the expense of others. While using government to corrupt the economy is as old as human history, the founding fathers tried to build protections that they hoped would keep the American market free. For about a hundred years, their plan worked. The US had the least corrupt economy that had ever existed. That began to change when federal, state, and local governments tried to boost growth by encouraging railroad development. From the 1830s until the early 1870s, state and local governments expanded their practice of chartering roads, bridges, banks, and other undertakings. Leaving these enterprises to the private sector would have led to slower but more sustainable development.

Government officials seem reluctant to trust the market when they should and are quick to trust it when they should not. These governments intervened in transportation by granting special charters and subsidizing the railroad industry. The evidence indicates that corrupted capitalism began with the late nineteenth-century railroad barons learning to take advantage of government largess to increase profits. The railroad barons began seeking political solutions to increasing competition, resulting in increased regulation favoring some groups and harming others. This regulation resulted in an unequal playing field that showed those in business that enlisting government intervention in the free market could be a successful route to profits. So they could succeed without earning it if they had the state legislate success for them.

Following the Civil War, the United States experienced a massive railroad boom fueled by government investments, rights-of-way, and land grants. However, as with most booms, this one led to a bust. The railroads were overbuilt, and cutthroat competition was driving rates to collapse. The consequences were stark. Shippers in Atlanta and St. Louis had a choice of twenty competitive routes, with distances ranging from 526 to 1,855 miles. The high cost of building railroads, both in terms of track and rolling stock, was offset by the early railroads' outsized returns. This created an expectation that the builders could easily recover these initial expenses. This unfounded optimism led to more building, intensifying competition, and driving down revenues. But the time it took to play out perpetuated the delusion of easy profits.

This time lag created a classic system dynamics scenario called overshoot and collapse. It occurs in population growth, resource management, inventory maintenance, and many other situations. It also describes most boom-and-bust cycles. A time lag separates rapid supply growth and slower-growing demand in these systems. In this case, the supply is the railroad system, and the slower-growing demand is the number of customers available.

As the railroads grew, they satisfied customer demand faster than new customer creation. Over time, this led to desperate competition for the existing customers and rates fell. This rate collapse meant the railroads' projected schedules to make back their investments fell apart. Track mileage increased from 105,000 miles in 1879 to 141,000 miles just three years later, with no corresponding increase in the customer base.[9] This overbuilding forced rates down further, so the railroads cut expenses, including wages and capital expenditures, which dampened economic growth. This cost-cutting led to the deepest, most pervasive, and most sustained depression in American history.

As damaging as the depression was, it had a lingering, even more damaging effect. Populist and progressive demands to solve the problem that the government had created fueled the rise of government economic intrusion and the welfare state in the following years. Strikes and riots erupted, and federal troops were dispatched to quell them. The resultant violence killed dozens, including thirty in Chicago in July 1894.[10] All this is because of the corruption of free-market capitalism by the government.

This depression caused the first serious challenge to the idea that the government is responsible for ensuring a fair, level playing field for the markets and protecting the citizens from internal and external harm. It turned the country away from the founders' concept that the government's job is not to meddle in the economy but to create an environment where the people can do great things. Once these railroad barons had "broken the ice" and diverted the law from its true purpose, an ever-increasing cycle began as others began to see the advantages of exploiting the law as a financial tool. This realization led directly to lobbyists who only used the government to realize their ends. In addition, these railroad barons became the poster boys for the "greedy capitalist" when the government should have been blamed.

So capitalism is being blamed for, what, governmentalism?

That's a great word. This "governmentalism" does even more serious and hidden harm. As damaging as rent-seeking and corrupted capitalism are to the economy, more severe damage occurs beneath the surface. This is the damage that results from the harm done to the reputation and understanding of capitalism and free markets in the public mind. On the one hand, the government corrupts capitalism by its actions and, on the other, blames capitalism itself for the ensuing corruption. The government's failures to control monopolies, tinkering with wage and price controls, and corrupting capitalism to benefit a few at the expense of many have created public pressure to change the US economic system. The current pressure to transition the United States toward socialism is a failure of governments, not markets. A free market includes freedom from corruption.

> The current pressure to transition the United States toward socialism is a failure of governments, not markets. A free market includes freedom from corruption.

Would socialism do better? There are good reasons to believe otherwise, and it has become critically important to answer whether socialism can result in greater economic good than can be achieved by spontaneous order, as is created by the combination of individual choices that make up the free market. Furthermore, the repeated failures of socialism may indicate that fundamental socioeconomic principles prevent their success. For example, my published research has proved that it is impossible to forecast economic variables with sufficient accuracy to allow a centrally planned economy, like socialism, to result in greater economic good than can be achieved by a free market.

But capitalism and the free market can certainly be improved. Many people are too quick to blame the "greedy capitalists" for their attempts to curry government favor. All people—all living organisms—pursue their self-interest. The cells in the human body keep us alive and well by pursuing their self-interest. Still, when the process runs amok in the form of cancer when cells pursue their self-interest in ways that are detrimental to the body, the person harmed must take action and use medical treatment to eliminate the threat.

Failure to act is the individual's fault, not the cancer cells'. Similarly, one of the government's most important duties is to prevent persons or groups from pursuing their self-interest at the expense of the populace. If the police stop enforcing laws, the resulting rise in crime is the government's fault. Left to themselves, most people will pursue their self-interest harmoniously, but some will pursue it as vigorously as they are allowed. In the same vein, most capitalists and entrepreneurs provide necessary goods and services at fair prices, but the government is to blame if it doesn't hold those who cheat accountable.

The government has necessary and legitimate purposes, the

most important being mutual protection. Corrupted capitalism is theft disguised as simply doing business. Free markets encourage competition, which in turn provides incentives for companies to create better products and services. These markets lead to economic progress, which will benefit society. All of us working to provide the best quality of products and services we can for one another makes us all the more likely to flourish and grow.

Government intervention is necessary as long as that intervention is to prevent other actors from unfairly altering value. Only free markets can establish fair value. The government must use economic policy to keep those markets free. They must intervene to prevent companies, unions, foreign governments, state governments, or anyone else from interfering in the action of free markets setting fair value. Failure to do so harms the entrepreneur, like the braider, Kine, and her potential customers.

These abuses of power could be eliminated by adding this amendment to the US Constitution.

Section 1. The fundamental right of citizens of the United States, as active participants in the free market, to freely negotiate value with consumers stands inviolable. No government or other agency shall artificially set or influence the value of any product or service, including labor, thereby ensuring the citizens' freedom to determine economic worth.

Section 2. The right of citizens of the United States to securely and freely conduct lawful business and trade is a cornerstone of our society. This right shall not be infringed by the provision of assistance to any private enterprise.

Section 3. The right of citizens of the United States to freely conduct lawful business and trade is protected. However, certain exceptions exist. The requirement of qualifications or fees is permissible, but only when directly associated with using government property such as roads. For instance, a state may require commercial drivers to demonstrate competency and pay licensing fees to use public roads or operate a business in a public park.

Section 4. Nothing in this amendment shall be construed to prevent states from effectively legislating against all forms of business and trade fraud, including but not limited to false declarations of qualifications to deliver a particular product or service. For example, someone treating patients and claiming to have a medical degree to qualify them is committing fraud, as is someone falsely claiming to have two years of training as a beautician.

What about forms of corruption not driven by money?

So far, we've discussed corruption in terms of money. However, money is by no means the only gain sought by corrupters. Those pressing for undue influence also do so for power, status, and recognition. Here's what may be the most egregious example of corrupted capitalism as measured by the direct effect on the people. In the 1950s, the American Heart Association invested millions in heart disease research. It was the beginning of a story that led to one of the most seriously flawed results of federal intervention ever produced. The results were a disaster that continues today, almost seventy-five years later. It is the story of Dr. Ancel Keys and the American diet. Keys was an example of using cronyism to seek power and status rather than money. He is also an example of professionals using their high status based on intelligence and talent, rather than money, to achieve their ends. Credentialed expertise is second only to wealth in the ability to exert undue power and influence.

Washington, DC, took notice of the disease that was "suddenly" striking the rich and powerful after President Eisenhower suffered a heart attack. As Washington is prone to do, a mentality of "we have to do something or at least appear to" began to take hold. As often happens, United States Department of Agriculture (USDA) and National Institutes of Health (NIH) officials quickly fell under the spell of "experts" who offered quick, easy solutions. In 1961, Keys, who had no nutrition science or cardiology training, got himself and an ally onto the American Heart Association nutrition committee. Keys had a hunch that saturated fat and cholesterol were influential factors in heart attacks and strokes. Without evidence supporting that position, Keys persuaded the committee to include recommendations for reasonable substitutions of corn or soybean oil for saturated fats.

Later that year, *Time* magazine, in the ultimate status reward, featured Keys on the cover along with his advice to cut dietary fat down to 15 percent of total calories.[11] The rest of the media picked up the ball and ran with it. Study after study failed to provide evidence to support Keys's claims, but his outsized reputation kept him from being discredited. At the same time, other researchers produced credible research indicating that not fat but carbohydrates were the actual culprits.[12]

The bottom line is that Keys's hypothesis is not true; the government and the media have brainwashed almost all of us to believe that eating too much saturated fat is responsible for elevating our cholesterol levels and increasing the risk of heart disease. The government has told us to significantly reduce our consumption of red meat, dairy products, eggs, and salt. These unfounded claims have been part of school health classes for decades. The media constantly reinforces the same claims. The USDA and the NIH have assured us these are facts supported by extensive scientific evidence. As a result, the Food and Drug Administration (FDA) and many state and local governments have taken steps to try to limit public consumption of these fats.

Where's your evidence?

I'm glad you asked, because the USDA, NIH, FDA, and media's claims are bogus nonsense if you examine the evidence. A large study published in the *Annals of Internal Medicine* concluded that saturated fat does not cause heart disease.[13] Just like virtually every research effort in the past half century, this one confirms there is no evidence that the saturated fats in butter, cheese, and red meat, demonized by the government, should be avoided. The studies do not show that dietary cholesterol increases serum cholesterol and is responsible for clogging our arteries. It is propaganda generated by self-serving pseudoscientists, status and power-seeking frauds, as well as politicians pandering to the food industry, anxious to sell more and more junk food to addicted consumers. Study after study has shown that the sugars in processed foods are more addictive than cocaine. Yet the food industry lobbies hard to prevent the government from taking too hard a line on them.

However, there is some good news. An article at sciencealert .com reported on December 20, 2024, that "FDA Rewrites Rules of 'Healthy' Foods for First Time in 30 Years."[14] Among the major policy changes were the movement of eggs into the healthy category, acknowledging recent confirming evidence that dietary and serum cholesterol are not linked,[15] and the movement of white bread and some other simple carbohydrates out of the healthy category. Finally.

Furthermore, nutritionist Dr. Luise Light, one of the primary creators of the original Food Guide Pyramid, has spoken freely about the corruption that dramatically altered the Food Pyramid created by folks who knew something about nutrition.[16] She reports that the USDA nutrition panel, on which she served, recommended five to nine servings of fruits and vegetables, three to four servings of whole grains, and sparing amounts of "baked goods made with white flour—including crackers, sweets, and other low-nutrient foods laden with sugars and fats."[17] After review by the Secretary of Agriculture, these recommendations were edited by the Secretary's office and replaced by two to three servings of fruits and vegetables, six to eleven servings of whole grains, and advice to avoid too many highly processed junk foods rather than the original recommendation to "include them sparingly." While both phrases are somewhat vague, the food industry insisted on these changes to preserve their most profitable products.

What were the results of the public being sold this lie? An epidemic of obesity has been prevalent since the 1980 USDA release of its Dietary Guidelines for America. As of 2023, the latest year for which official data is available, almost 40 percent of adults in the United States were obese, nearly double the 1988–1994 period when just over 22 percent of adults were obese.[18] This epidemic results from ignoring the objective evidence that a diet high in simple carbohydrates rather than a diet high in saturated fats is the most significant factor in causing obesity and heart disease.[19] In the final analysis, the United States government may be responsible for the millions of early deaths of people who trusted that their government knew what it was doing and told them the truth about what food was healthy and what food was not.

Unlike what those pushing an agenda would have you believe, there is no ideal diet. It is delusional to think a 300-pound Olympic powerlifter and a 110-pound yoga practitioner should make the same dietary choices. One size rarely fits all. We are all different, with different lifestyles, genetic make-ups, exercise habits, and sleep patterns. As you know, I'm an economist, not a nutritionist, but I know how to research. That's what everyone needs to do for themselves.

If you are a powerlifter, look on weight-lifting websites and see what diet the lifters most like you use. If your main exercise is yoga, see what folks like you eat to be successful. After that, experiment; find out what works or doesn't for you. One general rule that almost all nutritionists agree on is avoiding processed foods, particularly simple carbohydrates and sugars. They say it more directly than "include them sparingly." They say these foods should not be a part of a healthy daily diet. Sure, have cake and ice cream on your birthday, but not every day. Nutritionists also agree that the higher the quality of food you consume, the better.

Won't some people always pressure the government to take actions that will help them achieve their goals?

That's true. Some like to blame "greedy capitalists." But remember the scenario we posited earlier. Someone is burglarizing your home and you call the police, and the police offer to help the burglar. They help him load his car with your stuff. Of course, the burglar did wrong, but the police did far worse.

Sometimes corruptors are after money, but that's not all that corrupts capitalism; it's a lot more complicated than that. It may be status, notoriety, position, or self-satisfaction. Large organizations, like governments, are prone to a one-size-fits-all way of thinking. It's not always wrong, but finding situations that have worked well is difficult. Any large organization is not monolithic. All of these organizations have a diversity of opinions within them, and the voice you hear today is undoubtedly only one of many opinions held in that organization and is frequently incorrect. This skepticism is essential when the government speaks because governments have more control over your life than other entities. Cronyism, corruption, and ignorance contaminate not only free-market capitalism but every aspect of government, including areas as personal as diet. So keep your head on a swivel and your eyes wide open.

> **If the nature of change and economics were simple enough to explain on a bumper sticker, everyone would better understand it.**

If the nature of change and economics were simple enough to explain on a bumper sticker, a billboard, or in a thirty-second commercial, everyone would better understand it. It's taken us quite a while to get this far, and there's still more to come.

SUMMARY: What Is Crony Capitalism?

We showed how government tinkering with the economy exploded the cost of health care. We discussed how the government has allowed monopolies to take over industries without serious challenge. We also talked about how governments pass laws to help increase the profits of certain industries—like Arizona and the cattle industry.

We also touched on the corporate veil and how the government makes rules that allow corporations to be shielded from responsibility for their actions. For example, if you own a dog and it bites your neighbor, you can be held legally liable, but if your company harms your neighbor, only the company can be held liable. That's like saying your neighbor can only sue your dog because the pet owner's veil protects you. This veil is a corruption of capitalism by the government. It is not a failure of the free market.

As a result, many frauds and manipulations go undeterred. This leads to and encourages lobbying, which is an overt attempt to corrupt the government for personal gain.

We discussed the case of Kine Gueye, who, despite having a successful business and a loyal clientele, the state believed was a danger to society because of unregulated hair braiding. Kine was only a threat to established beauty shop owners who sought to eliminate the competition and enlisted the government to do their bidding. It's crucial to remember the government's primary role is to protect the public from such bad actors, not to aid them.

We also discussed the history of corruption beginning with the poster boys for greedy capitalists—the railroad barons. We showed that the government was far more guilty than the barons because the barons had no duty to the public, but the government had the duty to prevent their actions and failed. This was an early example of how capitalism is often blamed for governmentalism. To prevent these abuses of power, an amendment to the US Constitution could eliminate them.

Corruption is driven by more than money—fame, prestige, revenge, and a desire to dominate others all play a part. We discussed a large study published in the *Annals of Internal Medicine* that debunks the bogus idea that eating fat makes you fat. The government used this misguided notion to promote dietary guidelines that may have caused millions of premature deaths but got Ancel Keys on the cover of *Time* magazine, illustrating how factors beyond money can play a part in corruption.

Free-market capitalism relies on government to police the market and keep it safe from wrongdoers, just as you rely on the government, or should be able to, to protect your person and property from criminals. When the government fails, the government is to blame, and we must hold the government accountable and not let it transfer the blame to the wrongdoers. They will always exist, and one of the primary roles of government is to keep them in check.

Much of the negative perception of capitalism stems from attributing government failure to market failure. Some localities have decriminalized shoplifting, resulting in increased shoplifting. Blaming all capitalists because the government aids and abets the bad behavior of some is no different than blaming innocent customers for the acts of the shoplifters instead of the government that decriminalized it.

[8]

What Makes
Capitalism Succeed?

Free-market capitalism succeeds far beyond any other system for many reasons. We've already talked about some of them. It succeeds because spontaneous order can adjust the economy as necessary far faster and more accurately than any planner could—like a flock of birds that turns in unison with no leader and faster than a leader could have directed. Free-market capitalism succeeds because entrepreneurs are motivated to devise and market services and products that grow the economy. We used the analogy of a pie. Capitalists don't make money by taking a bigger piece of a pie that is a fixed size. Instead, they make money by growing the pie bigger and taking some of the extra and leaving bigger pieces for everyone.

Free markets succeed because the power lies with the consumers, the people. The people have all the power because they vote with their choices, which are even more empowering than free elections because choices trump voices. They literally put their money where their mouths are. They are free to express their self-interest in pursuing their values by how they allocate their resources. Free-market capitalism eliminates exploitation because no one has power over anyone else except as dictated by the government. Furthermore, capitalism is the expression of hope. Capitalists in the economy and every area of life invest resources today for a better future. Unlike any other system, it has evolved naturally whenever people have had the freedom to allow it to develop. This economic powerhouse is the driving force behind the benefits of the modern world.

Capitalism has been the savior of the world, at least in the economic sense. This achievement is evident when we examine two related data sets. First, Figure 3 vividly illustrates the world's gross domestic product (GDP) for the last two millennia. This data, the GDP, measures the total value of goods and services produced by the world economy in a single year, measured in inflation-adjusted dollars. In the year 1 AD, the world's GDP was about $213 billion. In 2024, the top five US companies each produced more than the entire world two thousand years ago. In the year 1000 AD, world GDP had risen about 15 percent to $245 billion—a thousand years and no significant progress.[1] Free-market capitalism, the catalyst of economic progress, has single-handedly rescued the world from centuries of stagnation.

By 1500, the GDP had increased to $500 billion, but it was still less productive than Amazon is today. However, the entrepreneurial spirit that introduced free markets and capitalism to the

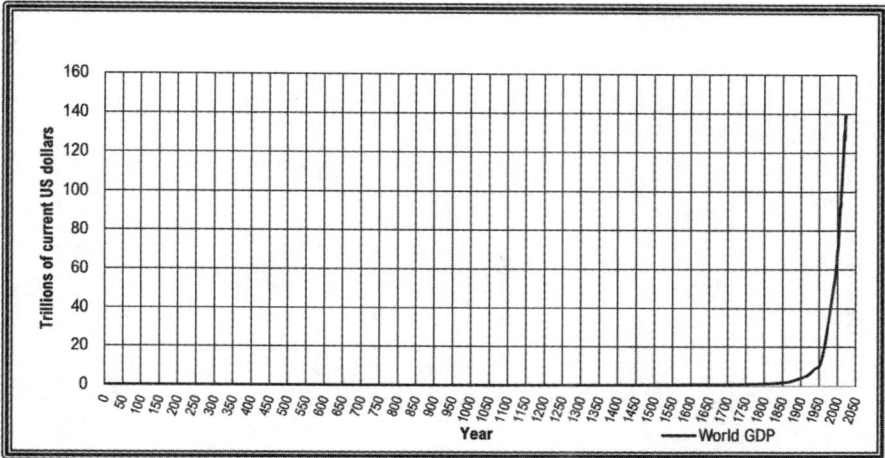

Figure 3. World GDP in history

world economy around 1600 rapidly improved production. For the first time in history, capitalists began to invest in increasing production. By about 1800, a new nation had been born dedicated to those free markets and capitalist investors, and in the century from 1700 to 1800, world production doubled, much due to a booming US economy. Since then, the United States has led world economic growth so that today, the world GDP is over 650 times greater than in 1 AD and 185 times as productive since the American economic boom, as shown in Figure 3.[2]

Figure 4 shows an even more informative view of progress: GDP per person. This graph shows that some of what looked like progress in our first graph was an illusion created by population growth. From 1 AD to 1000 AD, GDP per capita actually decreased. By 1500, the world was still worse off than in the year 1. After 1,500 years of economic stagnation, it was finally, slowly, brought to life in 1600 with the birth of free-market capitalism.

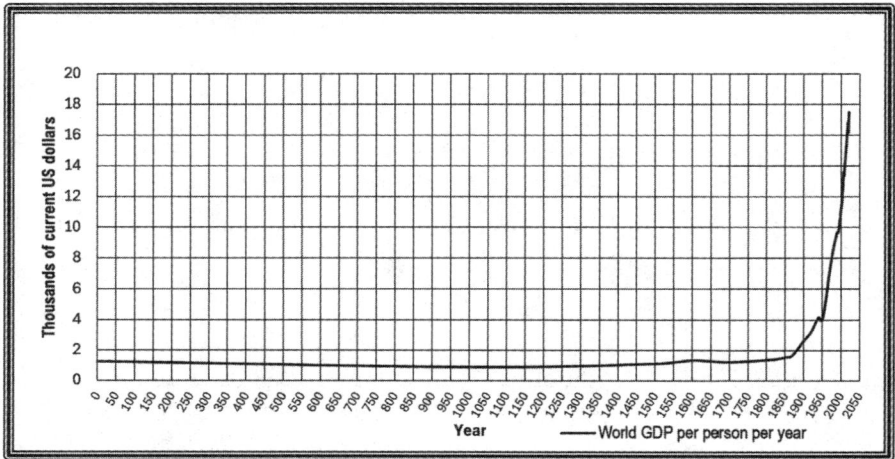

Figure 4. World GDP per person

From 1700 onward, there was no turning back. In 1776, a new nation was born, the first nation founded on free-market capitalism. This new nation's economy boomed like no country's ever had, and the world's economy came with it. The world's prosperity, propelled by the dynamic growth economy in the United States, continued to accelerate.

Today, the average human is twenty times better off than a thousand years ago and fourteen times better off than four hundred years ago. The numbers are even higher in the United States and much of the more developed world. This enrichment is the power of free-market capitalism. This system is not just for the elite but also for making the world better for everyone, driving global economic growth, and improving lives. Free-market capitalism, a system that has not just lifted but catapulted billions of people out of poverty, is a global force for good. In 1820, a staggering 76 percent of the world's population lived in extreme poverty. Today, thanks to the transformative power of capitalism, fewer than 9 percent do.[3] Those who oppose capitalism may not realize it, but they are advocating a return to a fixed, no-growth economy in which everyone suffers. Capitalism, on the other hand, benefits everyone, making the world a better place for all.

You've talked about crony capitalism; is that the only force that interferes with capitalism?

Corrupted capitalism is not all that the government does to disrupt the market. Another offender is the establishment of a permanent codependent welfare state. A welfare state is essentially a codependent relationship between the government and the populace. It is a means of controlling the citizenry and maintaining a hold on power. Those who advocate for an expanded welfare state believe that segments of the population are inadequately equipped, by birth or by circumstance, to cope with the demands of day-to-day living. However, those in power, or who wish to be, recognize that appealing to these advocates can be used to gain and retain control. They have found that creating codependent government programs accomplishes those ends.

Codependents are also known as "enablers" because they allow those who depend on them to continue engaging in unhealthy behaviors. Codependency is a dysfunctional relationship dynamic in which one actor assumes the role of "the giver," sacrificing their own needs and those of others for the sake of the dependent, "the taker." As a result, codependents do harm disguised as good to satisfy their own emotional needs.

Socialists are prone to label those who disagree with them as mean and heartless but attempting to end a codependent relationship is by far the kinder position. Codependency does not help people; it is a destructive behavior that only exists to satisfy the emotional needs of the enabler. Enablers exploit others and cripple those they purport to be helping.

But doesn't welfare help a lot of people?

Current welfare schemes help some but harm many. The welfare state policy expansions that began in the sixties have done generations of harm to Black families while the enablers applauded their own virtue. Unfortunately, they've succeeded in portraying their ego satisfaction as a noble effort to improve minorities' lives. Despite overwhelming evidence that their programs created more harm than good, they have continued the ruse, ignoring evidence.

The left's power elite, the architects of these policies, are particularly guilty. Their actions are not accidental and unintended; they are an inherent part of their plan to take and hold power. Just as any codependent exercises power over the dependent with the threat of cutting them off, these power elite do the same thing.

First, they provide funds, let's say, for education, and then they use the threat of removing those funds to enforce policies important to their agenda. They have employed the same tactics throughout the federal agencies. They can accomplish this by convincing Americans who want to help others that these programs are well intended and will successfully solve problems like poverty. However, the evidence says they cannot.

According to the Census Bureau, the family poverty rate was 8.8 percent in 1973; since then, it has been as high as 12.3 percent in 1993, during the Clinton administration, and as low as 7.8 percent in 2019, during the Trump administration. The fifty-year average is 10.3 percent. In 2022 the family poverty rate was 8.8 percent, exactly where it started fifty years prior.[4] Fifty years of spending billions to achieve nothing.

Are those who advocate these positions lying? I don't know who's lying and who is honestly mistaken, but these enablers have misled millions of caring Americans who truly believed these enablers' schemes were helping people. Hopefully, these millions will learn the truth over time and see that however pure their motives are, the enablers have manipulated them into encouraging harmful policies. Furthermore, we hope they will come to believe that all people have worth and can succeed on their terms if the government no longer enables the behaviors that have kept them from achieving their dreams. Most of these programs have proven to be a waste of our tax dollars. Now is a perfect time to discuss the source of those tax dollars: taxes.

What about taxes? Are the rich paying their fair share?

Let's consider an analogy. Imagine a hypothetical short hike in a beautiful part of Hawaii. The trail is nice, wide, and flat and is surrounded by incredible sights. It's one mile out and one mile back and suitable for hikers of all fitness levels. At the farthest point, there would be a break for lunch. This trip includes one hundred hikers, each allowed a ten-pound pack.

When you arrive at the trailhead, you learn that the group voted and, by a slight majority, had decided that all the hikers' packs would be redistributed so that the fittest hikers would carry the most weight. The hikers had completed a fitness test the week before that consisted of the total squats, push-ups, and sit-ups each could do in one hour. Organizers looked at data from previous research and found that the fittest individuals could score almost 11,000 on the test, and the least fit averaged 0. They found this fitness inequality concerning and decided to try to equalize it; after all, the fittest could carry more, so it's only fair that they should carry more, right? They averaged the scores into six categories and used a fitness formula they had designed to distribute the total weight of the packs among the hikers. The total weight of all the packs was 1,000 pounds.

Their formula would distribute the weight, rounded to the nearest pound, as follows: The fittest individual scored 10,000 on the test and would carry about 423 pounds. The next four scored 3,200 and would have around 51 pounds. The following five scored 1,000 and would take approximately 22 pounds. The next fifteen scored 200 points and would carry about 10 pounds. The next twenty-five averaged 75 points and would carry roughly 4 pounds. The remaining fifty hikers averaged 33 points and would take about half a pound.

Let's pretend you scored 3,200 on the fitness test and would be required to carry 51 pounds. How do you feel about that? That's one hundred times the amount carried by the least fit fifty—that's too much. You object, saying that you work out at least an hour a day between running and weight lifting, so why should you be penalized for your hard work?

The group spokesman responds that this is necessary to overcome fitness inequality and that it is fair for the majority to rule. However, this so-called fitness inequality results from personal choices and could be easily rectified by the majority taking steps to improve their fitness level. In fact, by carrying less weight, the least fit are lowering their exercise level and increasing the fitness gap. Furthermore, by taking their original ten-pound packs, the majority would improve their fitness levels and begin to close the fitness gap. Also, by overloading the fit groups, those carrying extra weight are given much more exercise, increasing their fitness level and thereby increasing the fitness gap.

It's also unfair for the majority to rule in a manner that harms innocent minorities. Would it be fair for the majority to vote to force the more-fit hikers to carry not only most of the weight but the less-fit hikers as well? Can the majority vote to discriminate against any group they choose? Since they decided to penalize healthy people, can they also decide to penalize tall people, or are tall people exempt because they were born that way and fitness is a choice?

It is essential that, as a society, we find answers to these questions because this story is not entirely fiction. In fact, it is a direct analogy to the American tax structure. The six groups and the amounts they must carry are identical to the US tax brackets. Higher incomes are much like fitness, since both result from choices and actions. Like the fit hikers who devoted resources to achieving their fitness level, those with higher incomes spent time, money, and educational expenses acquiring skills and abilities that have increased their income level.

So the rich actually pay more than their fair share?

Contrary to what you may have been repeatedly told, the information I just shared is not a fabrication. It's based on the 2023 United States Income Tax data, a reliable source you are welcome to verify. According to this data, the top 1 percent of earners contribute a substantial 42.3 percent of all taxes collected.[5]

Making some people carry or pay more is a form of majority-dictated slavery. It is forced labor disguised as fairness. Forcing anyone to work for someone else's benefit is the very definition of slavery. The majority dictating it does not excuse it; it simply makes the majority slaveholders. The principle is beyond any moral justification. If you agree with these tax policies, you are an enslaver. Income is the result of work; taking money earned by labor is no different than taking the labor itself. It is forcing someone to work for someone else's benefit. It is a disguised, indirect form of slavery.

> ## Making some people carry or pay more is a form of majority-dictated slavery. It is forced labor disguised as fairness.

That doesn't mean that all taxes are theft. Only unequal taxes are theft, stolen from the minority by the majority with no logical or moral justification other than having more votes. Members of the majority who vote for persons who promote unequal taxes become enslavers. People make choices; those choices have consequences. Each person has to own their choices. We call that personal responsibility. We say, "What goes around comes around," or we call it karma. In fact, in various phrasing, it's a central tenet of all the world's major religions. It has been a fundamental concept in law since Hammurabi's code in 1755 BC. Justice demands that all people get what they deserve. A vital part of that concept is that everyone is responsible for the results of their choices and actions, for better or worse.

What's the answer?

Everyone must carry their fair share of the burden in hiking or taxation. Fair share can only be determined by equally dividing the load rather than punishing those who have made the best choices and acted on them and rewarding those who have made poor choices. Furthermore, allowing the majority to target minorities cannot be tolerated. Everyone deserves equal treatment under the law regardless of the "will of the majority."

The easiest way to do that would be a national sales tax that exempts groceries, as most states do. The infrastructure is already in place since states and municipalities have already done it. It would cost far less than the IRS and would be a tax on consumption, not income. That is, the biggest spenders would pay the biggest share. This plan changes the burden from what people have earned to taxing how they spend their money. Those pursuing extravagant lifestyles would pay more taxes because they spend more money. Taxing income is tantamount to taxing success.

Politicians often oppose the idea because it's much easier to sell raising taxes on the rich. People have a hard time resisting getting something for nothing or getting someone else to pay the bills, so the majority votes for politicians who push unfair taxes.

Why don't we just tax the corporations?

Let me give you a bit of background on corporations. Corporations are a way for a group of people to share company ownership. They do this directly by buying shares of stock or bonds. Also, indirectly, by purchasing mutual funds, insurance, putting money in a bank account, or saving in an IRA or other retirement plan. If you do any of these things, you are investing in corporations. That is, you are directly or indirectly sharing in the corporations' profits.

Unlike the family farm and the corner shop, large undertakings such as an automobile or drug company require vast amounts of money to get started and to fund new growth. Risking that capital justifies the profit investors like you receive in dividends and appreciation. No one will take the inherent risk without the hope of reward. If no one takes that risk, most of the benefits that provide us with the goods we want will disappear.

Every organism, including people, pursues their best interests. The "greedy capitalists" people complain about are people just like you who make money from investments. Corporations use all that money invested directly or indirectly by shareholders like you as capital in creating new products and services. The investors, the capitalists, are rewarded with profit. In the case of stockholders, the child who receives one share of IBM stock as a Christmas present earns the same percentage of profit as the largest shareholder. That child is one of the capitalists who own IBM.

Although, the largest holder of IBM stock is the Vanguard Group. This mutual fund company has more than twenty million investors in 170 countries. Anyone can buy shares in a Vanguard fund for $1,000 and, through this fund, own stock in IBM and hundreds of other companies.

A board of directors manages a corporation and hires a chief executive officer (CEO) to oversee the day-to-day operations on behalf of the stockholders. The directors and the CEO are bound by what is usually called the business judgment rule. The business judgment rule is a legal doctrine that helps protect a corporation's board of directors and CEO from frivolous legal allegations about how it conducts business. The rule says that corporate managers are presumed to act in "good faith" within the standards of loyalty, prudence, and care that directors owe to stakeholders like you. Therefore, absent evidence that the board has blatantly violated some rules of conduct, the courts will not review or question its decisions. This protection applies while the board and CEO follow fiduciary standards.

It's more straightforward than it sounds. Fiduciary standards include "the duty of care" and "the duty of loyalty." The first is an obligation to act after due diligence to allow acting in an informed manner. That is, directors have a responsibility to perform due diligence as to the possible consequences of their actions before taking any action. The second requires directors to put the interests of the shareholders before their interests or those of others. This rule prevents corporate officers from taking any actions that do not directly or indirectly benefit the stockholders. For example, they can donate to charities in reasonable amounts to obtain goodwill that may ultimately benefit the stockholders. In addition, they can contribute to political campaigns to influence public policy to benefit the stockholders. However, the contributions must be limited and justifiable.

So corporations are not allowed to take any action not in the best interests of the stockholders?

Exactly, and the result of all this is that when the government taxes a corporation, the corporation cannot reduce stockholders' profits for people like you, unless there is no other choice. However, there is always another choice: passing the tax cost onto the consumer—that is, raising prices. This price increase, in turn, has two effects. First, it essentially taxes the consumers and does so as a "flat tax"; that is, it taxes all consumers the same percentage. Second, it places American companies at a disadvantage compared to foreign companies that are not taxed. So foreign companies can charge less for the same product, which forces American corporate downsizing through layoffs and wage reductions for American workers.

So you might say it's like the sales tax I suggested earlier, but it causes layoffs and wage reductions that would not happen under a government sales tax. It's impossible to tax corporations; it is only possible to levy a hidden tax on consumers. The general public believes that the tax is being paid by the corporation, but those in the know recognize that only the consumer pays the tax. As a result, the stockholders end up harmed in two ways. First, since they are also consumers, everything they buy from American corporations costs more. Second, they will likely have lower dividends and lower stock appreciation. If no one benefits, why do it? The politicians want to make it seem like they can give you stuff without you having to pay for it. It's a scam.

The government and the media also misrepresent corporate earnings to convince the public that taxing corporations is a good idea. The most common way they do this is by reporting the change in profits rather than actual profit. For example, imagine a company making a 1 percent profit annually. Now imagine that the corporation increases its profit to 2 percent in the next year. The profit rising from 1 percent to 2 percent is an increase of 100 percent. However,

2 percent is far too little profit to attract investors in a market where 7 percent is average. Reporting the 100 percent increase in profit rather than the meager 2 percent actual profit is misleading. It is a device that allows the government to continue scamming the public into believing that taxing corporations benefits them. It does not. When the percent increase is reported, the reader is led to believe that the company is making huge profits, which is used to generate calls to raise corporate taxes. Via the percent increase—a meaningless statistic to the general public—the media manipulate the public into a false conclusion: that companies are making huge profits. The average net profit for the S&P 500 companies for the last hundred years is about 7 percent, but a given company may make more or less. For example, let's say a company reported a profit of 11.29 percent, better than the S&P average but hardly excessive. However, that was an increase of 519.7 percent from the previous year's profit of 0.02 percent. So the average for the two years was 5.7 percent, well below the S&P average. Reporting the increase rather than the amount makes it seem to most that they are making an exorbitant profit rather than a modest one.

Since you are likely both a stockholder and a consumer, you are paying the tax when a corporation is taxed. It is the duty of those who understand this travesty to help educate those who don't understand. It is long past time to end this practice. As citizens, consumers, and investors, we must urge the government to eliminate all corporate taxes and to instead tax us directly with a sales tax rather than hiding taxes by funneling them through the corporations. Such a change would also lower overall taxes by eliminating the corporate expense of the record-keeping and legal work that these taxes require. If we eliminate corporate taxes and the progressive income tax, everyone would have more money because there would be far less waste. If we correct this injustice, only self-serving politicians would have cause to regret it.

The politicians have convinced enough voters that the government has magic powers. These politicians have convinced them that the government can deliver an inexhaustible supply of whatever they want. It has convinced them that it knows everything and can do anything. They believe the government can wave its magic wand to create a world of sweetness and light where everyone will have everything they want and bask in happiness. Everyone needs to understand that for every dollar a government spends, the government takes from someone else, which creates many of the problems the politicians claim to be solving.

Doesn't capitalism create inequality? Don't the rich get rich and the poor get poorer?

Two factors create the impression that free markets create inequality. The first is the part of your question that asks if the rich get rich and the poor get poorer. Well, that's not exactly true, is it? The rich keep getting richer, but the poor are getting richer as well, but more slowly. The poor today are much better off than the poor fifty or a hundred years ago and vastly better off than millennia ago. Some believe the rich are getting rich by exploiting the poor. But are they?

Let's change the context a bit and test that idea. What if we said, "Runners get better at running, and nonrunners don't get better"? Would that surprise anyone? Would it imply that runners were doing some hidden evil to gain running skills at the expense of nonrunners? Runners improve because they run a lot, and non-runners continue to let their running muscles atrophy and may even get worse. The rich get richer because they have invested time and effort in learning how to manage money effectively, and the poor don't do as well because they haven't developed these skills. Another way of making our original statement would be, "People who manage money well gain money, and people who don't manage money well don't." Now, said that way, it's obvious, isn't it? Of course the rich get richer, and the poor, not so much.

How can it be unfair that a person who runs half an hour daily is better at running than someone who never runs? It would seem that it would be substantially more unjust if the person who never ran magically could run as far and as fast as the practicing runner. Would it be more fair if everyone got the same results no matter what they did? No karma, no justice. The mass murderer, the rapist, or the racist all get the same treatment as the physician, the scientist, or the artist. Are those who favor these policies hoping for a world where no one is responsible for their actions?

Is money any different? How do you make a small fortune without getting good at handling money? Start with a large fortune! Lottery winners prove this every day. Winning a million dollars doesn't get you money skills; it just gives you more to mismanage. And mismanaging money is a sure way to end up without any. Just like fitness, in which the fittest keep getting fitter, but the least fit do not improve at all. That's because the scale is one-sided. It goes from zero to infinity. So the upper end is free to increase, and the lower end must stay the same. This one-sided scale means the spread will constantly be increasing. That is, the gap between the fittest person in the world and the least fit has been continually widening throughout human history.

You said there were two factors. What's the other one?

The more powerful reason is that the perception of inequality boils down to innovation. Innovation tends to happen cyclically, and right now, we are in the midst of this type of cycle. So the question is, why does inequality happen, and why in patterns? Significant innovations usually precipitate it. Examples include the first industrial revolution, the second industrial revolution, the agricultural revolution, and the current computer revolution. These innovations divide the populace into relatively well-off early adopters and those who cannot afford or resist the shift. The two groups exist in tension. While separate, they are connected as if by an invisible rubber band. As the early adopters forge ahead and the rest of society lags back, the tension in the rubber band increases. It stretches as the two ends get farther apart. Those who employ the new technology gain productivity advantages and increase their income, creating income inequality.

The second industrial revolution is a good example. This revolution, which began in the late 1800s and ended in the mid-1970s, resulted in the rapid increase in the use of assembly lines to create consumer goods. These cycles take a long time to manifest. Thirty or forty years after the beginning, income inequality peaked during the late 1920s. Those investing in assembly lines, such as Henry Ford, made huge profits. At the same time, the benefits of assembly lines had yet to reach the average consumer. In addition, many workers were forced into lower-paying jobs. The rubber band was stretched tight, but inequality began dropping as the benefits of assembly lines became more widespread in US households, and workers began to retrain for the higher-paying jobs the new technology created. The thirty years between 1950 and 1980 was a time of some of the lowest inequality in history. The rubber band pulled the top and bottom closer by raising the bottom. But it also created substantial societal changes.

During this time, households experienced an unprecedented increase in functional wealth. Functional wealth is wealth measured in the improvement of quality of life. The boom of household appliances, refrigerators, gas and electric stoves, home heating and air-conditioning, washing machines, and dryers gave the average household the equivalent of four or five servants one hundred years earlier. These machines were a factor that freed women to enter the workforce if they chose.

Around 1977, a new revolution began—the computer revolution. The same pattern repeated as the rubber band started to stretch. Like Ford, half a century earlier, early entrepreneurs of this new technology, like Gates and Jobs, made fortunes. Businesses and individuals who bought computers enjoyed a competitive advantage and increased their income.

As in the past, workers were slow to retrain, resulting in lower real wages and thus increasing the inequality gap. This new technology was expensive. An entry-level computer like the TRS-80 cost about $2,900 in 2022 dollars. Only the well-off could afford this new technology, but as they bought more, the companies used the income to lower prices and research ways to improve. As computers improved, more workers lost their jobs, and many had to retrain. Inequality increased. However, because the early adopters bought into the technology, the funds to improve and make it less expensive meant that computers have become more and more affordable and powerful. Table 1 compares the TRS-80 with a modern desktop computer and an inexpensive cell phone. The table shows that, while crude and expensive by today's standards, this early computer paved the way for society-wide benefits.

I had one of those TRS-80s. We thought it was terrific. In many ways, it could outperform the mainframe—which filled half the room—we had at the office. But, by today's standards, it's a paperweight. And that's precisely the point. Financial inequality drove the progress. I was one of the early adopters and undoubtedly gained an economic advantage by using a computer others could not afford. Without initial inequality, innovation would be impossible.

Innovation usually leads to some form of automation. An obvious current example is the increasing use of self-checkout lanes in stores we discussed earlier. It was predictable. The recent push for

Table 1. Comparison of a TRS-80, a desktop computer, and a smart phone

	TRS-80	Modern desktop	Improvement over TRS-80	Google Pixel 7a phone	Improvement over TRS-80
Price	$2,900	$2,899	Equal	$444	Less than 1/6
Processor speed	1,780 Hz	5.4 billion Hz	3 million times	~2 billion Hz	Over a million times
Memory	4,000 bytes	32 billion bytes	8 million times	8 billion bytes	2 million times
Storage	50,000 bytes per cassette tape	1 trillion bytes	20 billion times	128 billion bytes	2.56 million times
Monitor	11 × 8 in., black and white, 64 × 16 characters, no graphics or sound	24 × 19 in., millions of colors, hi-resolution graphics and sound	5 times larger	6 × 2.8 in. or the size of connected monitor, millions of colors, hi-resolution graphics and sound	1/20 up to millions with connected monitor
Added features	None	Mouse, Wi-Fi, Bluetooth, video and audio playback, video and audio recording with optional mic and camera, editing software		Wi-Fi, Bluetooth, front and rear cameras, video and audio recording and playback on both, video editing, sensors: proximity, light, accelerometer, gyrometer, magnetometer, and barometer	

dramatically increasing the minimum wage forced a price rise that the consumers were unwilling to pay. The higher prices did not provide the customer with a higher level of service, so they sought alternatives. Generally, two options typically present themselves: automation and outsourcing. Outsourcing supermarket checkout hardly seems practical, so retail businesses are choosing automation. Stores, to keep prices down, tried self-checkout lanes. Customers complained but chose lower prices, so self-checkout lanes became more common.

Is that the voices or choices idea we discussed earlier?

Exactly! People often complain because they don't adjust well to change. It's uncomfortable. It's unfortunate that self-checkout means cashiers must change jobs. No one likes to see people's lives disrupted, but it is a natural consequence driven by consumer choice. For example, scanning and bagging groceries saves time in checkout lines. Some say we should do away with this automation and keep the checkers. Still, the idea here is to create value for the consumer and society. If the idea were to create more jobs, that's easy. Keep the checkers and make them all work with one hand tied behind their backs. That would provide many more jobs. But why stop there? Let's eliminate the checkers' scanners and return to manual cash registers. Then there would be even more jobs. But at what cost? We would be devolving instead of progressing.

Furthermore, as we talked about earlier, why stop at checkout lanes if it makes sense to eliminate self-checkout technology? Why not eliminate all innovation? The wheel certainly put lots of people out of work. The wheel allowed one person with a wheeled cart to transport the same loads half a dozen people could carry, eliminating the jobs of the other five, but led to new careers in wheel-making and cart design as well as chariot building. Luddites—innovation protesters—have made the same kind of argument against every innovation you can think of. Do we want to return to the caves and refuse to allow any human progress in the name of protecting jobs?

Of course, no one wants to see people put in the position of changing jobs or even careers, but this is the only way to improve society in the long run. Change isn't always better, but better always requires change. In our example in Table 1, in only fifty years, computer technology improved from being something the majority could not afford to computers and cell phones being available to almost everyone. Now, 98 percent of the US population has cell phones, and 91 percent have smartphones that are millions of times more capable than the first TRS-80, for one-sixth of the cost.[6] All innovations that only some can afford initially help innovators figure out what consumers want and are willing to pay for.

If early adopters had not purchased those TRS-80s, the computer revolution would have stalled, and there's a good chance we would have missed out on the benefits we enjoy today. The rubber band that connects the early adopters and the rest of society stretches tight, increasing income inequality, but then contracts to pull the rest of society to a much better place. All of the innovations we enjoy today began with the well-off. We originally only found microwaves, VCRs, DVD players, televisions, automobiles, air-conditioning, electric lights, and much more in upscale homes. Take a mental trip through your house and think about what you see. How many items were available only for the well-to-do at one time? How many meant someone had to change jobs?

I see what you mean. Almost everything in my house put someone out of work at some time in the past, didn't it?

I'm sure all of you saw something similar. Eliminating the effects of the inequality rubber band means eliminating the rewards that inevitably follow—for everyone. One proof of this is the shrinking middle class. Yes, it is shrinking. Since 1971, 4 percent have moved into the lower class, but twice as many have moved into the upper class.[7] This increase in upper-income folks will almost certainly drive the next wave of human progress. The inequality rubber band is a crucial ingredient of human progress. A world without income inequality would be dead, with no improvement or growth. Every innovation requires a paradigm shift that changes fundamental aspects of society. People are often loath to embrace change, but change is the only element of life that never changes. The only constant is change.

Marx thought this change and progress was too disruptive to be allowed. Part of his reason for advocating his plan, socialism, was to prevent change and progress. Marx was wrong. The only thing we can do to make things better is to embrace change and help others deal with it—it's the human thing to do.

> **Free-market capitalism succeeds because every member of society is motivated to seek the rewards capitalism offers.**

Free-market capitalism also succeeds because every member of society is motivated to seek the rewards capitalism offers. No other economic system offers the economic upward mobility that capitalism does, and most allow none. Most people in the world today still have no hope of improving their condition by their own effort. Most can only hope that their nation or the world will improve enough to incidentally be of benefit to them. Free-market capitalism is the economy of hope.

SUMMARY: What Makes Capitalism Succeed?

It's the natural way. Capitalism relies on spontaneous order to regulate the economy rather than the government. This gives the consumers the power. They make the economy change depending on their purchasing. No one forces anyone to do anything. It is true freedom.

Free-market capitalism is responsible for the greatest increase in human well-being ever. Thanks to free markets and capitalist investors, worldwide extreme poverty is nearly eliminated and being reduced further every day.

Free markets steer clear of codependent relationships. Free markets don't try to encourage or discourage consumer choices the way the government does. Free-market capitalism performs best when taxes are fair and equal. The government uses unfair taxes to make some groups slaves to others. Capitalism rewards entrepreneurs for their efforts to improve life for everyone and recognizes that taxing companies is just a devious, hidden tax on the people. Unlike what many believe, capitalism creates equality. It gives everyone a fair chance to create value for others and to profit from it.

Capitalism doesn't put people out of work. The progress it creates sometimes alters the employment landscape, but everyone benefits in the long run. Capitalism means innovation and progress because it allows choices to trump voices. By that I mean the choices people make are often at odds with what they are voicing. However, it is their choices that truly express their values.

We also showed the myth that the rich don't pay their fair share of taxes is false. Using the analogy of hikers carrying packs, we learned that the rich are paying far more than their share. Everyone must carry their fair share of the burden in hiking or taxation.

Then we exposed the detrimental effects of taxing corporations, which ultimately becomes a flat-tax burden on consumers and harms the economy. This practice also provides an unfair advantage to foreign corporations exempt from the tax, further exacerbating the issue.

We also exploded the lie that capitalism breeds inequality. Free-market capitalism is, in fact, the great equalizer. It provides everyone with an equal opportunity to create value and potentially achieve prosperity. The government, however, often worsens inequality by meddling in the economy, causing the impacts of innovation to be sudden and disruptive, rather than gradual and adaptable.

The ultimate testament to the superiority of free-market capitalism is that while some may complain it's unfair, they continue to enjoy its rewards. Everyone's house is full of products that put people out of work. Is anyone advocating boosting employment by giving up all job-killing, labor-saving devices?

Capitalism is an investment in the future. It is an economy of hope and applies to all choices. Exercise, education, saving, planting a garden, purchasing tools, buying a home, and anything else that looks to the future are capitalist activities.

[9]

What Makes Socialism Fail?

W hy socialism can never work is one of my favorite topics, since this subject has been a large part of my economic research. The direct answer is that the economy is a chaotic system interrupted by bubbles and black swans. Let's take one part at a time. Economics is a chaotic system. The easiest way to understand chaotic systems is to consider the weather. The weather was the first chaotic system analyzed to the degree necessary to achieve understanding.

You've probably heard of the butterfly effect. A weather researcher named Edward Lorenz originally coined the phrase to describe an essential attribute of chaotic systems. A defining characteristic of chaotic systems is that tiny input changes can lead to colossal output changes. Lorenz titled one of his research presentations "Predictability: Does the Flap of a Butterfly's Wings in Brazil Set Off a Tornado in Texas?"[1] I know it sounds crazy but imagine an extensive weather system beginning to form and needing only a tiny nudge to activate it fully. Enter the butterfly. It's like the straw that broke the camel's back.

That is why weather reports are so inaccurate; after a decade of study, researchers realized that the weather would only be helpfully predictable up to two weeks in advance. Suppose you have doubts— experiment. Every day for a week, check the forecast in your favorite weather source and write down the basic facts for the weather a week ahead. Then, wait a week and compare the actual results with the predictions. Two nights ago, where I live, it was supposed to get down to nineteen degrees. I spent a few hours preparing plants and water sources for the upcoming freeze and another hour preparing my travel trailer so the pipes wouldn't burst. After I finished, an updated weather report said the overnight low would be thirty-one. None of the work was necessary. That was a twelve-degree differ- ence, just a few hours apart. I'll bet you've had similar experiences. Why socialism can never succeed is in large part due to the fact that, like the weather, it is a chaotic system.

Are you saying that economics is a lot like the weather?

I'm glad you asked. Yes, chaotic systems, like the weather, exist when millions of independent elements combine to create a but- terfly effect, as shown in Figure 5. Weather is caused by moving air and water; every movement by people, animals, insects, and fish moves air or water. To accurately predict the weather, knowing how all these actors are and will be moving would be necessary— clearly, an impossible task.

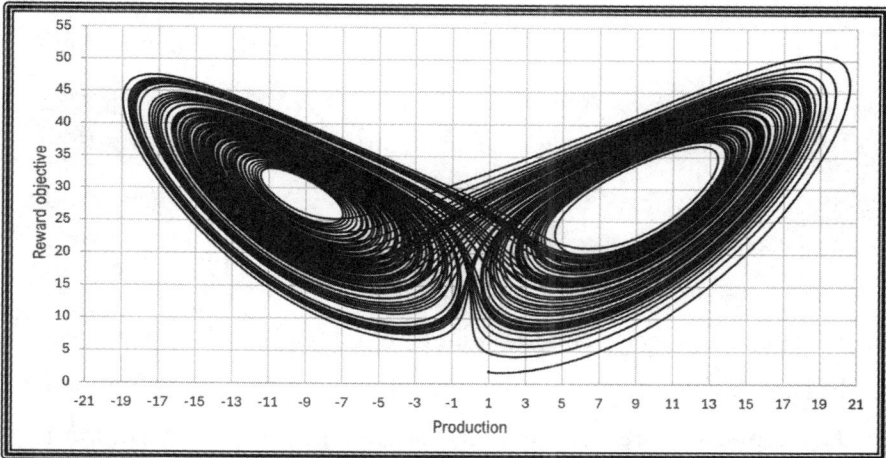

Figure 5. The interaction between production and reward

Figure 5 shows one of many ways of modeling chaos. When Lorenz first planned to publish his findings, he originally thought to use a seagull flapping its wings, but the distinctive shape of one of the graphs he was using gave him the idea of using a butterfly instead. This graph is based on one of many economic theories that all produce essentially the same results. It shows how the desired reward varies with the amount of effort the individual, company, or government exerts toward attaining that reward.

In most graphs you can go to any point on the horizontal axis and find a single corresponding point on the vertical axis. This is how models make predictions. However, in the butterfly effect graph, we can immediately see the problem: Choosing a point on the horizontal axis doesn't give us a single answer but dozens. Any of those results is a possible outcome of the point chosen on this axis.

That is the nature of chaos. Each execution slightly changes the input of the next execution, which alters its outcome. The same would be true if there had been a slight change in the original input, the butterfly flapping its wings or a producer working a bit harder today and increasing their output and therefore changing their reward objective. While this explanation is somewhat simplified, it makes the difficulty clear. Predicting the economy is impossible, rendering long-term economic plans virtually worthless.

The economy is a chaotic system. Today, eight billion people are buying, selling, saving, and consuming. Therefore, making accurate economic predictions requires knowing what each person is doing economically and their financial plans. Like the butterfly effect in weather, a shopper buying a pair of shoes in Peru could be the tipping point that triggers a recession in Poland.

In North Korea, there is a black market. Every controlled economy has always developed a black market because people want what they want and will find ways to get it. Black markets are much more than butterflies; they are elephants that produce severe economic distortions.

You said another factor was bubbles. Is that like the housing bubble in 2007?

Exactly. Chaos is one of many problems that make economic predictions unreliable. The second is "bubbles" or boom and bust cycles. Speculation by large numbers of inexperienced investors causes markets to overheat beyond actual value, resulting in a crash. This sort of bubbly behavior has happened dozens of times—for example, with the the tulip mania bubble in the

Netherlands in the 1630s, the Great Depression in the 1920s and 1930s, and the housing bubble in 2007–2009. The results can be economically devastating, and no one can forecast them until it's too late.

Finally, the third disruptor of economic predictions is the "black swan." Black swans are unpredictable events that have wide-reaching effects. The recent COVID-19 pandemic and the resulting economic collapse are examples. But other examples include terrorist attacks, meteorite strikes, volcanic eruptions, and severe earthquakes. My published research indicates a 56 percent probability that at least one of the three factors will cause a consequential error in any economic prediction beyond the immediate future.[2] You would literally do better flipping a coin. Forecasts that are correct 44 percent of the time are not forecasts but guesses.

Chaos, bubbles, and black swans, as well as the problem of not satisfying self-interest, explain why centrally planned economies (CPEs), based on philosophies like fascism, socialism, and communism, always fail. Central planning fails because it requires the ability to forecast. For example, in mid-twentieth-century Soviet Russia, the experts' five-year plans never succeeded because the expert predictions they relied on were unreliable.

Like the flock of birds we discussed earlier, spontaneous order reacts to change better. Millions of producers and consumers can independently order the economy without needing forecasts or direction. Just as a flock of thousands of starlings can navigate and execute rapid turns, climbs, and dives with no leader or central planner, free people in a free, uncorrupted market move that market in the most beneficial direction for all. Free marketplaces have provided greater good to more people than any other economic system.

Couldn't experts, using models, do a better job of managing the economy than relying on the randomness of the market?

Some claim to have economic models that are accurate, but they have yet to prove it. Let's think about it. We base everything we know on the past. But everything we want to know is in the future. And the world is constantly changing. The future is seldom the same as the past. It's a subject I am very familiar with; I've spent decades studying modeling. I'll explain without getting any more technical than necessary. The question relies on the assumption that economics is predictable. Planning anything in the future with certainty requires the ability to predict the future with equal certainty. To understand much of why socialism struggles, you need to understand models and the fact that everything is beyond human understanding, which is why we create models. People are modelers, but they often get it wrong.

Planning for the future is a necessary part of life, but it is essential to understand that, as Robert Burns said in his poem "To a Mouse," "The best laid schemes o' mice an' men / Gang aft a-gley." In his poem, Burns states that no matter how well we plan and prepare for something, something can always go wrong unexpectedly at any point in time. I'm sure your life has been upset by unforeseen events many times. Three of the most translated and read texts ever written give part of the answer.

The Bible says, "Ship your grain across the sea; after many days you may receive a return. Invest in seven ventures, yes, in eight; you do not know what disaster may come upon the land."[3]

Shakespeare's Antonio in *The Merchant of Venice* said it this way, "Believe me, no. I thank my fortune for it—, My ventures are not in one bottom trusted, Nor to one place, nor is my whole estate, Upon the fortune of this present year. Therefore, my merchandise makes me not sad."

Cervantes's Sancho in *Don Quixote* gave his answer as "Es parte del sabio guardarse hoy para mañana y no arriesgar todos sus huevos en una canasta," which translates to "'Tis the part of a wise man to keep himself today for tomorrow and not venture all his eggs in one basket."

All these admonitions include the assumption that the world is a chaotic place and advise diversification as a defense against chaos. Intentionally or not, these ancient texts advocate the advantages of a free market diversifying economic control by spreading the decision-making across millions of producers and consumers rather than a small group of expert planners in which all the eggs are in one basket.

But don't experts predict economic outcomes all the time?

Yes, but they are wrong more often than they are right. I have examined the data from the personal consumption expenditures from 1985 to 2015. It demonstrated failures in the three areas we've discussed. The chaotic nature of the economy, characterized by its sensitivity to initial conditions and the amplification of small changes, caused general errors. There were extreme errors attributable to boom-and-bust cycles, specifically the asset bubble of 1985–1987, the Nasdaq bubble of 1994, and the housing bubble of 2007–2008.

Finally, there was a black swan event, the pandemic of 2020–2022, which was responsible for the most significant errors in economic forecasting history. During the thirty years studied, the data indicate a 43 percent chance of chaos distorting the consumption projections severely enough to upset planning, a 19 percent chance of an asset bubble creating such a distortion, and a 5 percent chance of a black swan doing so. Combining these probabilities results in a 57 percent probability that at least one of these events will create a severe distortion in the consumption projection.[4] This result indicates that economic forecasting, at least as far as consumer spending is concerned, is no more accurate than flipping a coin. Planning based on these kinds of odds is unsound and likely to do more harm than good.

Let's look at it another way. Have you ever put together a model airplane or played with dolls? These are models or replicas of actual planes and people. Models are important. They help us understand a complex world on a smaller scale, be it a plane, human, concept, or event. In the case of economics, mental models make every aspect of our perception of the world understandable, just as they did when you were a child playing with dolls or a toy car, imagining what it would be like to be grown up or driving a car. By pushing the toy backward and forward, we see how the wheels of the car work. By emulating the adults in our world with dolls, we practice what it will be like when we are older.

While models help us understand concepts from a high level, even the most accurately created, anatomically correct doll is an incomplete model. It is a simplified representation of a person. It might be great to see how clothes will look on people or learn the basics of human proportions, but it is worthless as a tool to understand the circulatory system, for example.

But I've seen models that were accurate. So this can't hold true in all cases, right?

No. What you are speaking of is a copy. Anything modeled with complete accuracy in all aspects is no longer a model but a copy, such as a replica of a painting. As a copy, it loses its value of simplifying reality to make it easier to understand. Understanding the limited accuracy of models is important because virtually all people tend to extend their models beyond their effective range. For example, if you opened up the doll, you would see cotton and decide as a young child that all humans are full of cotton. Just as the example of the doll is an overextension of the model, it can also be a pitfall in economic forecasting, leading to inaccurate predictions and flawed understanding of complex systems.

But doesn't a good economy help everyone?

Yes, but that's an oversimplification of the issue, just like a model. Let's look at another example. A rising tide lifts all boats equally; however, the metaphor does not apply to a rising economy. A rising economic tide doesn't lift all boats equally the way a nautical tide does. A better nautical analogy would be "a strong tailwind propels all boats." This analogy (also a model) captures the notion that the extent to which a tailwind helps depends significantly on the size of the boat and sails used.

Small sails will not benefit a large boat as much as large ones will propel a small boat. The economy is not like a tide that has the same effect on all boats; it is more like a tailwind that affects boats based on the kind of boat. By the same token, people who are shocked when the promised economic benefit is not delivered equally blame the system instead of examining the real issue.

Instead, people who blame the system for not delivering equal economic benefits are looking at a model of how they *think* an economy should work, instead of how one actually works. Saying a tailwind advances all boats but differently—instead of oversimplifying a complex issue by saying a rising tide lifts *all* boats—clarifies that the problem is not with the wind (economic system) but rather the different sizes of boats (levels of investment and productivity). A strong economy will benefit investors and high producers more than noninvestors and lower-level producers, but everyone will benefit and be better off.

Similar to how one might wonder if formulas in the "exact" sciences, such as physics, are correct, economic formulas (another kind of model) are like all models—incomplete generalizations. Experts in the natural sciences using mathematical models are generally more successful than social scientists; however, even those mathematical models have failings, the same as an anatomically correct doll or car is an incomplete model. They are only partially accurate because they are simplifications.

The failure to thoroughly understand the present makes predicting the future impossible. Let's visit an example from physics about gravity. The equation, which is a mathematical expression of a model, predicts the speed of a falling object at a future time using the equation $V = V_0 + gt$, where V is the velocity of the object at any time, V_0 is the initial velocity, g is the acceleration caused by gravity, and t is time.

This formula appears simple enough; if you know V_0, g, and t, then you can precisely calculate V. However, the equation is more complex than it appears because it applies only at standard temperature and pressure in a vacuum. These conditions never exist in the actual world and provide only an estimated range of possible outcomes. Socialism does the same but on a larger scale; it is a model and an ineffective one at that.

But aren't some scientific models reliable? I took physics in high school and had to memorize lots of formulas like the one you just mentioned. Was my teacher lying about that?

No, not lying, but your teacher may not have stressed the limitations of that model or any model as much as necessary. As an engineer would point out, the model requires ideal conditions to be completely accurate, and those conditions don't exist in the world. That formula can give an estimate, sometimes fairly accurately, but it's never exact. This lack of precision is true of all models, including those in the "exact" sciences.

Depending on the circumstances, it may be possible to predict a 90 percent probability that a given object of a specific size, shape, and weight falling for six seconds in the air on Earth, with an initial altitude of 16,000 feet, with the barometric pressure being between 27.9 and 28.1 inches of mercury, and with the temperature being 62 degrees Fahrenheit, will be falling between 45 and 49 meters per second.

Given such a simple formula, you might wonder why the answer is so uncertain. The answer is that to make a more precise calculation possible requires more variables to be included in the formula. For example, every cubic meter of air through which the object falls includes roughly ten septillion molecules in independent motion. Each of them interacts with the others and the object in unpredictable ways.

To arrive at an absolute answer, you must, among other factors, be able to predict the position and motion of each of these septillion molecules. It would also be necessary to account for unpredictable temperature and pressure as the object descends. Without a complete understanding of the present, a more accurate prediction of the future is impossible.

This impossible requirement is essential to the accuracy of all models. A complete understanding of the present is required to predict future behavior. Don't get me wrong; the physics equation $V = V_0 + gt$ is a terrific model. It perfectly explains the relationship between velocity, gravity, and time, but its application to any specific situation will always be an approximation.

What about climate change? I've read that those models are settled science. Is that wrong?

Climate models suffer from all the same problems as models in general. Is the climate changing? Yes. Do we know all the variables affecting it and the effect each of them has on the climate? No. Anyone who reads a lot of scientific journals can tell you that new research is published daily that discusses previously unknown factors. And economic models are no better, because they are far less precise than those in the physical sciences. The reason for this is economics is the study of the individual choices and actions of about eight billion people. As a result, economic predictions are, at best, an educated guess.

Duncan J. Watts—a computational social scientist and author of *Everything Is Obvious*: *Once You Know the Answer*—described an experiment in which he asked a panel of experts to submit nearly a hundred predictions in their fields twenty years in the future. Twenty years later, he scored their results, and the experts had only done slightly better than random chance. Geoff Colvin's book *Talent Is Overrated* describes a meta-study that found when it comes to judging personality disorders, which is one of the things we count on clinical psychologists to do, the length of clinical experience said nothing about skill. Some of the leading researchers concluded the correlations were roughly zero.

Surgeons are no better at predicting hospital stays after surgery than residents (trainees) are. Colvin says, "In field after field when it came to centrally important skills—stockbrokers recommending stocks, parole officers predicting recidivism, college admissions officials judging applicants—people with lots of experience were no better at their jobs than those with minimal experience."[5] This research is more evidence that expertise and models may be overrated.

> **When large groups of people are involved, free markets will consistently outperform planned markets.**

Bang and Frith compared isolated decision-makers to interactive groups. The groups always performed better than the individuals. Researchers have found that "in the Wason selection task, a well-known problem of logic, only 10–20% of individuals give the correct answer, but this increases for groups to around 70%."[6] This is because when large groups of people are involved, free markets will consistently outperform planned markets.

James Surowiecki, in his book *The Wisdom of Crowds*, explained that decisions and predictions made by groups virtually always outperform those made by individuals. One of his examples involves the television game show *Who Wants to Be a Millionaire?*

If unsure about the answer, the contestant could use one or more of three "lifelines." One of these lifelines allowed the contestant to phone a friend who was an expert in the field, another removed two of the incorrect answers, and the third lifeline allowed the contestant to poll the studio audience. The first two lifelines did pretty well, getting the correct answer 65 percent of the time, but this was dwarfed by the poll of the studio audience, who got the correct answer 91 percent of the time.

So you're saying science is wrong?

Wrong is too strong. Science is littered with outdated, outmoded, and wrong answers. It is also incomplete and evolving and will likely be so forever. As we get better tools, we get better answers. Science is about trying to learn about the world. If we ever did discover all there was to know, science would cease to exist because we would have learned it all. Every day, we learn new things that modify or contradict previous knowledge.

The struggle is as old as mankind. Here's another example: Over several millennia, scientists had developed an intricate mathematical model of the solar system and the stars. It predicted the location of the heavenly bodies almost perfectly. This model was geocentric, placing the earth at the center of the universe with everything else revolving around it. Of course, now we know better.

Copernicus proposed a sun-centered solar system with fixed stars in a book released in 1543. Still, half a century later, only a dozen astronomers agreed with his theory mainly because, while more straightforward, it did not match the observations as well. In the early 1600s, Kepler developed mathematics that supported the Copernican view. Still, the tide did not begin to turn until Newton provided new insight by deriving Kepler's laws from a gravitational model in 1687. After another hundred years, it finally became generally accepted as fact. It took two centuries to change the model of the solar system. Science takes a long time to correct its mistakes because radical change is only possible with convincing evidence.

Here's another example. In the late 1700s and early 1800s, Malthus created models indicating the world would soon experience famine. In today's language, he said the population grew exponentially, with food supplies growing linearly. Of course, more than two centuries later, the world is better fed than ever in human history.

Remember when we discussed the debacle Ansel Keys caused in the 1960s? Keys hypothesized that saturated fat and cholesterol were influential factors in obesity, heart attacks, and strokes; his model was simple: Eating fat makes you fat. Without evidence supporting that position, the cover of *Time* magazine featured Keys along with his advice to cut dietary fat. Study after study failed to provide evidence to support his claims. However, his outsized reputation kept him from being discredited. At the same time, other researchers produced credible research indicating that not fat but carbohydrates were the culprit. The results of this mistake have caused thousands of early deaths.

But back to physics—then why are they called "laws" of physics?

In science, words like *theory* and *law* have particular meanings different from common usage. Many of the most popular ideas at the frontiers of theoretical physics have one thing in common: They begin from a mathematical framework that seeks to explain more things than our currently prevailing theories do.

Most physics today is based on two basic conceptual frameworks: general relativity and quantum field theory. While they both do an excellent job of explaining some aspects of physical reality, they are incompatible, and neither explains many observed phenomena sufficiently, such as dark matter, dark energy, or why our universe is filled with matter and not antimatter, among other puzzles.

As I said earlier, we must thoroughly understand the present to predict the future. But complex physics aside, we don't understand the present very well. In the case of weather, for example, to fully understand the present, we would have to know where every butterfly was and what it was doing. The same would be true of every other living thing. When you go outside and feel chilly, you are losing heat to the environment. That means you are changing the weather a little.

Economics may be even more challenging. Not only would you have to know everything about every economic transaction, but you would also need to know about all economic planning. That is, what every producer was planning to produce and in what quantities, and what every consumer was planning to buy and in what quantities. In addition, you would need a way to factor in the fact that all of these actors may change their minds at any moment. That's why "experts" aren't able to make more accurate predictions. It's not that they are doing it wrong; they just don't have enough information and never will.

There are different ways to make predictions. One is pattern analysis, and another is probability based on history. A Yale University experiment compared a group of students' ability to predict outcomes with the predictions of a Norwegian rat. The study involves a T-shaped maze with food at one end of the T's crossbar. The researchers randomly placed the food on one side or the other, but their process guaranteed that, on average, one side would have the food 60 percent of the time and the other only 40 percent. The rat did not take long to head for the 60 percent side almost every time and, therefore, succeeded in finding food 60 percent of the time. Rather than using a statistical method, which is essentially what the rat did, the students tried to find patterns or models that would allow them to predict where the food was, which resulted in their predicting the correct side only 52 percent of the time, so the rat won.[7]

Consider the case of the Space Shuttle *Challenger*; everyone by now knows that failed O-rings caused the disaster during a much colder-than-typical launch. NASA analyzed the previous O-ring failures by examining every case of a previous O-ring problem. It appeared from this data that O-ring failure was not well correlated with temperature. Based on this data, they decided to launch. However, if they had included the data from all flights, not just those with O-ring failures, it would have been clear that temperatures below sixty-five degrees Fahrenheit had a far greater probability of failure than those above sixty-five degrees. All flights that resulted in no O-ring stress were launched above sixty-five degrees.

> **People are not particularly good at predicting the future because they don't always know what data to use to make their predictions.**

If we were to design a T-maze for the rats based on total chance and put food on the above-sixty-five-degree side 16 percent of the time, labeled "launch," and on the below-sixty-five-degree side 84 percent of the time and labeled it "do not launch," the rat would choose "do not launch." The lesson here is that people are not particularly good at predicting the future because they don't always know what data to use to make their predictions. Even NASA gets it wrong sometimes, and they *are* rocket scientists!

I can see how chaos would be hard to model, but what about bubbles? Could you explain that?

Asset bubbles, a term used to describe a situation where the prices of assets, such as houses or stocks, become inflated beyond their intrinsic value, typically occur when inexperienced investors attempt to make quick profits by rapidly buying and selling these assets. The housing bubble of 2008 serves as a prime example. Like most investors in any market, seasoned real estate investors focus on long-term investments. However, in the early 2000s, less experienced investors began rapidly buying and selling houses—a practice known as "flipping." This trend, coupled with a government policy that offered more flexible home loans, led to a surge in housing prices.

Eventually, buying a home, waiting a short time, and selling it for a higher price without making any improvements became possible. As prices continued to rise rapidly, speculators could flip homes within a month, a week, or even a single day. Eventually, prices reached a point where regular homebuyers could no longer afford to buy, and the bubble began to burst, causing prices to fall. As a result, individuals who had purchased real estate at inflated prices found themselves owing more than the current value of their homes. This rapid collapse led to widespread panic, further driving down prices and ultimately triggering the Great Recession. How could a model have predicted this a year or two in advance?

That sounds a lot like what happened in the Great Depression in the 1930s. Is that true?

Yes, all asset bubbles result from speculation by folks hoping to make a quick buck rather than investing for the long term. A great example is the Nasdaq bubble around the turn of the twenty-first century. Figure 6 demonstrates what that bubble

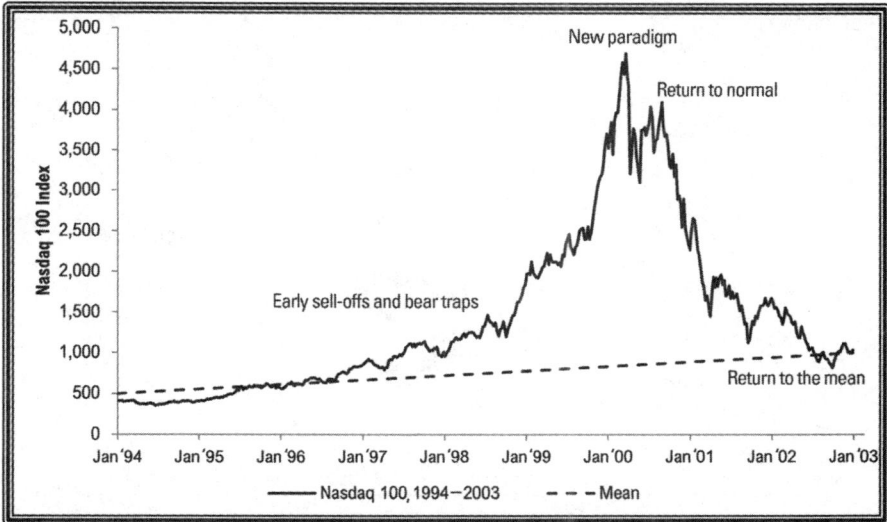

Figure 6. Nasdaq 100, 1994–2003

looked like. The labels are key inflection points that all bubbles have in common. From left to right, the labels highlight the withdrawal of the true investors, as opposed to speculators. The "New paradigm" point shows the sell-off by those who were part true investor and part speculator. The "Return to normal" point shows the peak caused by speculators seeing the prior decline as a buying opportunity and "doubling down." Finally, the "Return to the mean" point highlights the complete crash followed by a return to true value.

Figure 7 is another graph that shows the same points as Figure 6. However, this graph shows the composite stages in a bubble created by Jean-Paul Rodrigue in his book *The Geography of Transport Systems*. Rodrigue analyzed dozens of asset bubbles and described their commonalities.

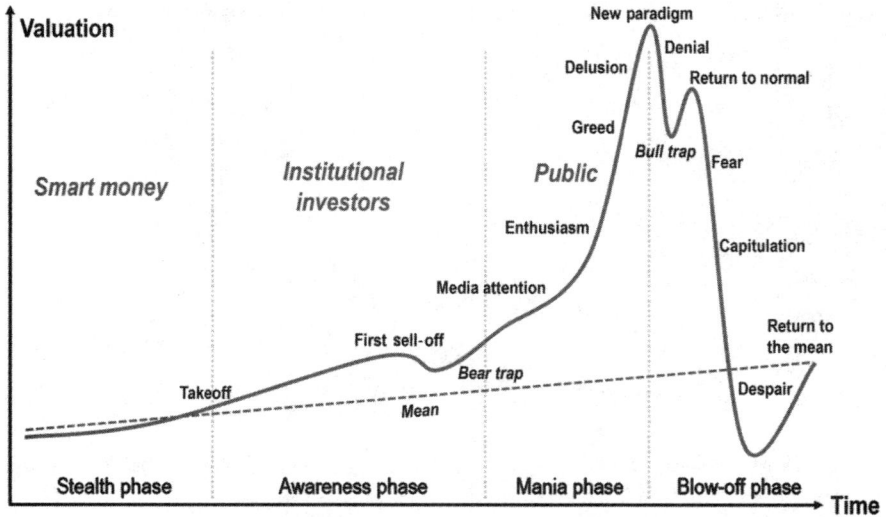

Figure 7. Stages of a bubble. (Source: Jean-Paul Rodrigue, "Stages in a Bubble," Geography of Transport Systems, accessed December 21, 2024, https://transportgeography.org/contents/chapter3/transportation-and-economic-development/bubble-stages/.)

I later created a mathematical model based on Rodrigue's assumptions that creates a virtually identical graph. Figure 8 shows my model that predicts asset price behavior based on speculator greed. It illustrates how increasing speculator demand drives up prices that eventually get so high the demand crashes, driving down prices. Notice that Figure 8 compares well with the previous two graphs, indicating that it is a good explanation of bubbly behavior.

Notice I said speculator greed. People tend to blame "greedy capitalists," but they are wrong; capitalists are not speculators. Yes, they put money—capital—at risk, but capitalists deal in long-term investments and are not trying to make a quick buck. They buy assets to provide capital for long-term growth.

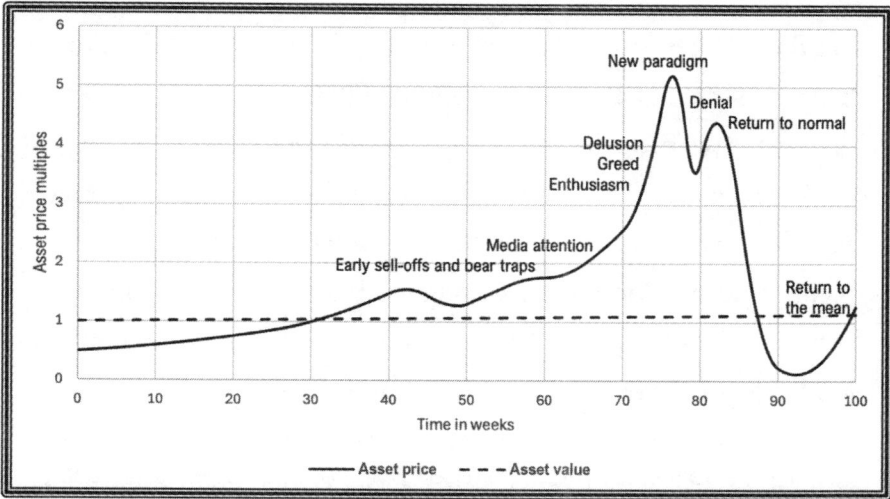

Figure 8. Asset price as a function of supply and demand over time

Asset bubbles occur when speculators, not capitalists, buy assets not to hold but to flip. It wasn't "fat cat capitalists" flipping houses but novice speculators trying to get rich quickly. Notice that in the prior graph, the capitalists—labeled the institutional investors—exited the market when the speculators came in. You can see from the Figures 6 and 7 and my model, Figure 8, that modeling bubbles after the fact, as I did, is easy but is impossible to do beforehand.

You said there was a third thing, "black swan," that also compromised prediction in the economy. What's that?

A black swan event is a rare, unforeseen event that got its name from the first spotting of a black swan bird, which was long thought impossible. Black swans are not economic events per se, but they can seriously affect the economy. Black swan events don't happen often, but like the pandemic of 2020–2022, they can be devastating to the economy and impossible to predict.

The complexity of economic forecasting is underscored by three significant factors: chaos, asset bubbles, and black swans. These elements render economic forecasting models ineffective beyond the very short term, typically two weeks to a month. Any attempt to predict beyond this time frame is akin to a random guess.

Of course, models do get better. They improve in short-term accuracy, but Lorenz—mentioned earlier as the discoverer of the butterfly effect—proved that chaos meant that no one could use models for weather predictions in the long term, and his proof applies equally well to economics. The economic models are also susceptible to asset bubbles and black swans. No economic models accounted for the 2008 recession, due to the housing bubble, or the financial devastation caused by the COVID-19 pandemic far enough in advance to be helpful. However, while experts using mathematical models can't make correct economic predictions and plan the economy, millions of producers and consumers who don't know anything about models and economics can do better than the experts because of spontaneous order.

Agility, distribution, and the wisdom of crowds, as seen in the free market, can adjust to changing conditions far faster than a CPE. Individuals and companies respond to changing economic conditions more rapidly than the government can. Furthermore, since the actions are distributed across billions of entities, what works rises to the top, and what fails sinks to the bottom. When the government reacts, it does so monolithically, putting all the country's eggs in one basket. Socialism is based on experts' ability to manage a nation's economy. Chaos, bubbles, and black swans make sufficiently accurate prediction impossible, and point to the resilience of free-market capitalism in such situations.

As we have previously discussed, free-market capitalism presents a robust solution to these challenges. It inherently provides insulation against chaos through diversification. Savvy investors constantly balance their investments, ensuring that if one sector falters, others will keep them afloat. This diversity, spread across millions or billions of people, helps maintain the stability of the economy by using the resilience of free-market capitalism.

What else does the market do better?

One of the critical issues is the government's role as a pseudo middleman to facilitate negotiations between consumers and producers. The government's intervention in this role often leads to unfavorable outcomes. Instead of allowing consumers and producers to negotiate, the government imposes its agenda, frequently exacerbating the situation. A prime example of this is the problem of student educational debt, a direct result of the government's intervention in the free market in education.

In the twenty years from 1997–1998 to 2017–2018, federal grant aid to college students in constant dollars more than tripled. Reliance on federal money removes the consumer (student) from the producer (educational institution). This separation constrains consumers from negotiating the value and price with the producers. Setting fair value is what free markets do best and what controlled markets do poorly. Separating consumer and producer tends to reduce smart shopping since, in this case, the consumer is not paying the product's total price. This absence of negotiation has the inflationary effect of allowing prices to rise without any accompanying increase in product quality. Subsidizing costs incentivizes rising costs. Public four-year institutions generally tend to raise tuition by double the amount of increased federal aid.

If the federal government provides an additional $500 in aid, the institution will likely raise tuition by $1,000. Educational institutions have no incentive to cut costs, and the evidence indicates that the cost increases are not devoted to improving instruction. In fact, in the past thirty years, instructional spending has decreased from 41 percent to 29 percent of institutional budgets. During that same period, tuition has increased eight times faster than wages.[8] Therefore, students thirty years ago who could, with a bit of help from their families, work their way through college with a part-time job are now eight times less likely to be able to do so, and many must rely on government aid or debt or both. Furthermore, those students thirty years ago would have had an increased percentage of institutional budgets devoted to their educations.

Let's look at the data from the *Digest of Education Statistics*. The acceleration of tuition cost increases, measured in 2023 dollars, began in 1980. While the cost of a public college education had been decreasing since 1963, a series of federal education expenditures began to reverse that trend around 1980. In that year, the average tuition cost per year was $2,196. By 1990, it had increased to $3,254, and by 2000, tuition was $4,385. Fast-forward to 2020, and the average cost of tuition had sky-rocketed to $8,695, a fourfold increase in forty years.[9] Since these figures are adjusted for inflation, they clearly demonstrate that the government's injection of money into the education system is a significant driver of cost increases.

Another example is health care. We discussed earlier how the government encouraged insurance companies to separate the producer from the consumer by using wage and price controls. There is no advertising by health-care providers seeking customers based on lower costs. The providers understand the consumer cannot comparison shop for less expensive alternatives. For instance, a patient needing a specific medical procedure may not be able to choose a provider offering the same service at a lower cost. This lack of consumer comparison shopping keeps the free market from adjusting prices based on value as measured by consumers, creating imbalances in the economy that other segments of the economy must correct.

So you're saying that one way to deal with economic chaos is to keep the government out of the economy?

Yes, you're right, except for retaining the role of the government in policing the economy to keep it free of corruption. The best solution for dealing with the chaos present in the economy is to allow the free market to do what it does better than any alternative: negotiate value between the consumer and the producer.

What about bubbles? Are there solutions for those as well?

Yes, let's take another look at the 2007–2008 housing bubble. Speculators flipping houses caused that bubble and the resulting crash. The homes weren't increasing in value; they weren't better. It was like a Ponzi scheme in which the initiators of the boom made profits, victimizing everyone else. Buying an asset, like a house, intending to resell rapidly to make a quick buck causes and worsens booms and busts. Legitimate investing does not cause asset bubbles; speculation does. Investors buying for the long term based on sound economics are essential to a thriving market. Speculation bankrupts most speculators and takes a toll on the economy, hurting millions of innocent bystanders. Again, it's not the capitalists that are greedy. It's speculators.

Given that greed fuels speculation, a problem we can't eradicate, it's crucial to find a solution that directly tackles this issue. The key is to remove the incentive for profiting from greed. A capital gains tax that favors long-term investment over speculation could be the answer. I propose a new tax law, the federal long-term investment protection tax, or FLIP tax, designed to do just that. This tax has the potential to stabilize the market, reducing the frequency and severity of booms and busts. It could also encourage more responsible investing, as the sliding scale tax rate rewards those who hold their assets for longer periods. The FLIP tax is a proactive solution that aims to discourage short-term speculation and promote long-term investment, ultimately benefiting the economy as a whole.

The FLIP tax, a fair and effective solution, is designed to

discourage short-term speculation and promote long-term invest-ment. And if it works as well as the design indicates it should, no one will ever pay it. This tax introduces enhanced protection for long-term investing and a substantial tax penalty for asset "flip-ping." This tax would necessitate reporting any investment asset buy, trade, or sale, including the date of purchase and purchase price of the asset and the date of sale and the asset's selling price. Most transactions of this nature already require this level of recordkeeping. From these records, the tax man can ascertain the hold time of the asset and the profit made in the transaction. The gain from the sale, if any, would then be taxed on a sliding scale. A potential formula for this tax could be $T = .75^t$, where T represents the tax levied on the sale and t is the time elapsed between the purchase and the asset's sale.

Figure 9 shows how it would work.

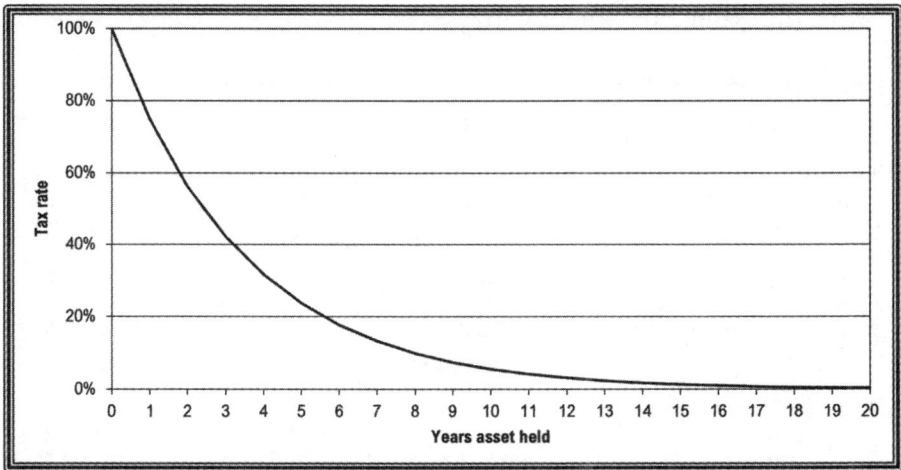

Figure 9. The FLIP tax rate by year

Flipping an asset after six months imposes an 87 percent tax on the profits. After a year, the tax is 75 percent. After five years, it's 24 percent. After ten years, the tax is down to 6 percent. At twenty years, it is less than 1 percent. Under this tax system, holding an asset for less than four years puts the tax rate above the highest marginal rate for ordinary income under US current tax law. Keeping the investment for between six and a half and seven and a half years would be necessary to get to the rates that current tax law allows after one year. After seven and a half years, the rate continues to descend until, at thirty years, it is essentially zero.

Do you have a chart that compares asset value under this new plan?

I do. Figure 10 shows how the investment would play out over fifteen years, assuming a normal 7 percent growth rate, compared with that same investment with no tax.

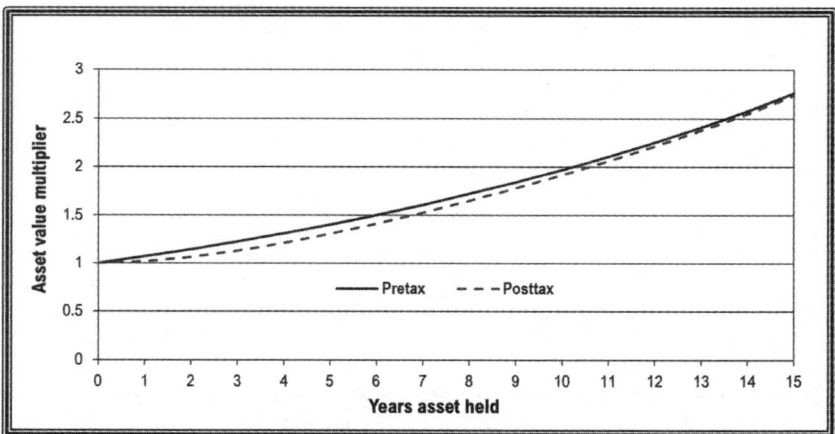

Figure 10. Asset value under the FLIP tax plan

The solid line is the asset's value without this plan, and the dashed line is the value after the FLIP tax is imposed. As you can see, the value after the tax is imposed makes the prospect of profiting by flipping assets quickly untenable. After about fifteen years, the tax has essentially no effect on the value. As you can see, the impact of the tax is to reduce profits for speculation and increase earnings for legitimate investing.

There are three tangible benefits of this FLIP tax plan:

1. It provides a massive disincentive to flip an asset. This tax would dramatically reduce, if not eliminate, speculation. Engaging in a highly leveraged and speculative investment would create an even more significant disincentive, since the tax raises the risk-reward ratio beyond acceptable levels.

2. It significantly increases the rewards for the long-term investor. Rewarding the long-term investor is essential because of its positive effects on the national economy and its guarantee to the investor of greater rewards. It also would benefit the average homeowner in that if they sold a home they'd held for a longer term or applied the proceeds from the sale of one home to another, as is allowed by current tax law, the profit from the sale would be tax-free.

3. The only way to eliminate market crashes is to eradicate the booms or bubbles. This plan does so. Some might worry that the tax early on is excessive; they might be concerned about the need to sell an asset in an emergency. However, this is not a cause for concern since the principle of the

investment remains whole; the investor can get their money back at any point since only the profit is taxed.

You can see in the graph that the asset value substantially decreased early on but narrowed to nothing as time went on. This tax is crafted in such a way as to make long-term investing more rewarding and flipping far less attractive. Since it mitigates greedy impulses, the FLIP tax is economically sound and can potentially improve morality by combating greed. In addition, it creates an even greater disincentive to engage in speculative investment based on borrowing or highly leveraged strategies as the risk-reward ratio is raised well beyond reasonable levels. It also has the benefit of dramatically increasing the rewards for those investing in the long term. This tax is a legitimate involvement of the government. It is protecting the citizens from the actions of the greedy few.

As a long-term investor, I love that idea, but how does it help the economy?

This advantage to the long-term investor is vital because it produces investor behaviors that positively affect the national economy. Even disregarding the potential for bubbles, speculation is of no economic value since it does not add value as investment does. The FLIP tax also brings significant benefits to the average person who is not actively investing. As mentioned earlier, it would treat a home as a long-term, tax-free investment when sold. It would also replace current IRA-type rules and essentially eliminate all taxes on retirement funds held for over thirty years. This means the average person's home and retirement savings would be tax-free, providing a substantial boost to their financial security. So the FLIP tax solves the problem of boom-and-bust cycles and benefits everyone. It keeps speculators from bankrupting themselves and others by creating a bubble that will ultimately burst. It rewards long-term investors for their productive use of funds. Finally, it benefits the national economy since the additional investment it spurs will promote sound economic growth.

It sounds like your solutions for chaos and bubbles could work. But what about black swans? How can you prevent the unknowable?

Good point. You're absolutely right. We can't prevent black swans. However, we can implement certain strategies. Humanity has been dealing with black swan events throughout history. We have never approached them by trying to forecast or prevent them since we recognize they cannot be predicted or prevented. Instead, humanity has always dealt with black swans by preparing for the worst—the first efforts involved storing food and supplies for times of drought or disaster. Later, wise folks created "rainy day" funds so the resources to deal with them would be available when tragedy struck. Today, many people prepare for disaster by stockpiling food. The Mormon church suggests its members store a one-year supply. In addition, many people have bugout bags and backpacks loaded with at least three days of provisions, ready to go in an emergency.

The most common modern preparation for black swan events is insurance. Most people have car insurance, health insurance, life insurance, and home insurance—all held in preparation for unexpected events. Of course, it is not practical for the government to purchase insurance, but it is feasible for the government to self-insure. For example, instead of borrowing to help the citizens in a pandemic, the government could create a special fund consuming 5 percent of the annual budget until at least six months of annual expenditures are acquired. Then, the government, like its citizens, would benefit from the additional security and from receiving interest on its savings. The government should prepare for disaster in much the same way its citizens do.

The government should also help individuals plan for disaster. One way to do this would be to create a savings program, much like an individual retirement account (IRA), that allows the individual to save money in an emergency preparedness account. This account would allow tax-free savings of up to two years' annual income. In the case of a qualifying emergency, the fund-holder could withdraw funds tax-free. This rainy-day fund could compensate for the loss of income due to a disaster, a health emergency, or unemployment; it would encourage people to prepare for emergencies. The income protection portion would convert to a traditional retirement account upon retirement. The remainder would pass to the holder's heirs after death, with the terms remaining intact for the recipient.

Shouldn't the government take steps to be prepared as well?

Absolutely! The government must do what its more prepared citizens do. Taking steps to prepare the government to mitigate the effects of a black swan event might include:

- Avoiding debt
- Living within its means
- Having plans for unlikely emergencies

The government's economic policy regarding black swans should mirror the wisdom of its citizens. The government's preparedness for black swans should be more like an enhanced version of the Federal Emergency Management Agency (FEMA) approach. Being prepared to address a crisis is superior to the Federal Reserve's managing the economic fallout after the fact. This approach is a testament to the citizens' foresight, and the government should heed their wisdom.

What about the really big things like global warming? How can capitalism help?

Great question! Not only can capitalism help; it's the only thing that can. Remember free-market capitalism is really just all the people in an economy cooperating. The public would like to see the problems associated with climate change solved, but they don't want their lives negatively affected by the solutions. An unhampered free market is the only practical answer.

Let's look at an example. Electric lighting uses about one-fourth of all the electricity consumed in the United States. A few years ago, the United States mandated a change to compact fluorescent bulbs (CFLs), and climate change activists cheered. However, the free-market capitalists, driven by consumer demand, responded with light-emitting diodes (LEDs) a couple of years later, surpassing CFLs in efficiency and popularity. This success story of LED lighting is a testament to the potential of free-market capitalism in addressing climate change.

The government's solution, CFLs (which, of course, was also created by free-market capitalists), and the market's choice, LEDs, both performed far better than the filament-based bulbs, but CFLs use 40 percent more electricity than LEDs. Switching from incandescent to CFLs would reduce US electrical consumption by 19 percent—that's huge, but switching to LEDs would reduce it by 21 percent. The free market wins again. As a bonus, LEDs have dozens of color temperatures and millions of color choices, while CFLs have one. Furthermore, LEDs are far less expensive over their lifetime. In 2024, an incandescent 800-lumen bulb cost $8.93 per year to use, a CFL cost $2.05 per year, and an LED cost $1.38 per year.

Here's why free-market capitalism works so well. The United States has about 330 million people, and about 260 million are adults. They all would like to have more money, so 260 million people are trying to find a way to strike it rich. They see that solutions to climate change would make them rich, so they look for answers. The US Energy Department has about fifteen thousand employees; if they come up with a solution, they may get a raise or a bonus, but they don't get rich. So the market has seventeen thousand times the number of potential entrepreneurs working on the problem than the government does, and since their potential for economic gain is far greater, they are far more motivated.

Capitalism still needs to solve the problem of climate change, but solutions take time. One big problem with government bureaucratic solutions is they are usually quick fixes. Politicians hoping to get reelected feel under constant pressure to fix things now, but that's not often possible. In response, the government throws money at the problem, damages the economy, and does things that don't work in the long run.

I've read that carbon sequestration might be the answer. Is that true?

It may be a large part of the answer. The highly motivated people I mentioned earlier are already discovering solutions that could be deployed in as little as five years. Carbon sequestration is definitely one of them. Carbon sequestration involves capturing CO_2 from the atmosphere and storing it somewhere safe. There are several possible techniques: growing crops to capture carbon and preserving and burying those crops is one way. Another method is injecting the CO_2 into rocks or water surrounded by rock. This process dissolves minerals that re-form with the CO_2 into new rocks that will last virtually forever. Old-growth forests store CO_2.

Using trees from old-growth forests in construction continues to store the carbon and replacing them with new trees allows more carbon to be captured. These innovative solutions, along with the potential of energy generation from air humidity, offer a promising future in the fight against climate change.

In addition to removing already present CO_2, scientists and entrepreneurs are finding unique new ways to generate and store electricity. Among these is one presented recently in the journal *Advanced Materials*, titled "Generic Air-Gen Effect in Nanoporous Materials for Sustainable Energy Harvesting from Air Humidity," which describes a process that uses nanopores in materials to generate electricity from the air.[10] Lightning is evidence of the vast energy stores in the air, and this discovery describes a method of extracting them.

But couldn't government experts do just as well or even better?

Look around your home for a moment. How much of what you see was created by capitalists, entrepreneurs, and free markets, and how much was created by the government? That's how free-market capitalism works. The solutions to climate change are coming soon as long as the government does not interfere—the way it tried to with CFLs. If you are worried about climate change, the only way to truly become a climate restoration warrior is to fight to keep free-market capitalism doing what it does best—letting people get rich by solving challenging problems for the benefit of all.

SUMMARY: What Makes Socialism Fail?

Socialism doesn't work, because planning an economy is impossible. Socialism, or any other CPE, is doomed to failure. Economics is a lot like the weather; it is unpredictable. Centrally planning an economy requires accurate prediction of future economic needs, which is an impossibility.

Three things make predictions inaccurate: chaos, bubbles, and black swans. Chaos exists whenever a very large number of independent, uncontrollable entities are able to effect large changes in a system with very small inputs—like the air and water molecules in the weather system of the billions of consumers in the economy.

Bubbles—boom and bust cycles—happen when speculators gamble on rapidly buying and selling assets in hopes of flipping them for a quick buck. All manner of assets have triggered these cycles. Tulips, stocks, houses, and other real estate have all caused crashes by the greed of flippers.

Black swans are unpredictable events that are so rare they were thought to be impossible, until they occurred. Pandemics, the various industrial revolutions, some inventions such as the wheel or paper, the 9/11 attacks, the sinking of the *Titanic*, the fall of the Soviet Union, and the European discovery of the western hemisphere are all examples.

Planning is based on models, and models are approximations. Therefore, all models are wrong. Some may be helpful in limited contexts, but none are accurate enough to predict the weather or the economy with helpful accuracy more than a couple of weeks in advance, and they never will be.

People think of the models used in science as being accurate, but they have limits like any model. Equations used in science are intended to describe and test relationships. They are not intended to make absolute predictions.

Free-market capitalism reacts to chaos, bubbles, and black swans faster and more effectively than any government can. Imagine a marching band—the entire formation can turn left instantly and move in a new direction. Now, imagine the band was on a huge trailer; it could not turn left nearly as quickly, since one large mass has far more inertia than a large number of smaller masses. In other words, millions of producers and consumers can react to change more nimbly than a monolithic government.

Socialism, whether you like it or not, cannot do the job of ordering an economy effectively. Every centrally planned economy has ultimately failed. None has ever survived even a hundred years—no time at all in the expanse of human history. Free-market capitalism has proven it can be effective in making life better for billions over many centuries.

[10]

Why Socialism Sucks

We've learned that socialism struggles because—along with its cousins fascism and the myth that is communism—it is an extreme system that requires a totalitarian government to implement it fully. In short, it struggles because it sucks. In Russia, China, the states in the former Soviet Union, Cuba, North Korea, and others, socialism only came into existence by military force. It was not by the choice of the people. And any system that is not the choice of its people sucks.

Socialism is not truly an economic system at all since economics is the study of choices, and socialism prevents the people from free choice. The state makes the economic decisions. Under socialism, there are no ABCs of economics, because people don't have the freedom to choose their actions and behaviors based on their choices. I'll say it again: A system that does not give its people free choice sucks.

Socialism also sucks because it prevents the consumer from deciding the value of things based on their own internal list of values. Instead, the state decides the price and the value of everything. Our values are a significant part, if not all, of our identities. And any system that denies our individual identity sucks.

Socialism also prevents the consumer from deciding the true value of labor. As with the value of things, only the consumer can determine the value of a service performed for them. When the state sets wages, it dehumanizes both the provider and the consumer. A system that doesn't let the people decide what a service is worth sucks.

Socialism interferes with free and fair trade. When socialists plan the economy, they place their version of what goods and services are desirable and limit the people's choices. Any system that imposes limits on the goods and services the people have access to sucks.

Socialism is anti–free-market capitalism. It denies entrepreneurs the right to help the people by creating new products and services to improve their lives. The struggles of people in socialist countries to obtain products from free-market countries are well known. And any system that doesn't allow entrepreneurs to create more and better products and services sucks.

Socialism not only sucks; it also cannot succeed because accurate economic forecasts are essential to plan an economy. We've learned that chaos, bubbles, and black swans make the necessary economic forecasting impossible. A system that is based on designing an economy from plans that are based on incorrect economic forecasts sucks.

In the end, socialism sucks because it is a lie—the biggest lie in history. It claims to be humanity's salvation, but instead, it has caused more death and destruction than any other single cause. It has killed hundreds of millions, imprisoned millions more, and reduced billions to poverty and life in a police state.

Socialism has killed more people than cancer, heart disease, and the black plague combined. It has imprisoned more people than all other incarcerating forces combined. It has held more human beings in police states that were little better than prison and kept more of them unfree and impoverished than all other forms of government combined. Nothing in history has caused harm even remotely close to this magnitude. Any evil you can imagine short of a worldwide thermonuclear war will never compare to the evil released by socialism. Lenin, Stalin, Castro, Brezhnev, Pol Pot, Ho, Hitler, Mao, Mussolini, Kim Il Sung, Kim Jong Il, Maduro, and dozens of lesser despots have released this hell in the guise of creating what Marx called the "workers' paradise." Marx was the author of the big lie, and these despots were his minions.

Even the names of the socialist states are lies. Here are their formal names: the Bolivarian Republic of Venezuela, the Republic of Cuba, the People's Republic of China, the Democratic People's Republic of Korea, the Lao People's Democratic Republic, and the Socialist Republic of Vietnam. None of these countries are republics or democracies. They are literally so in name only. Socialism requires dictatorship because socialism, by definition, requires absolute control over the economy, and absolute control over the economy means absolute control over everything.

And the final lie is that it would make its people happy. Even if it could succeed, I can't imagine anything less attractive, less fulfilling, and less progressive than a homogenous world where the state grants everyone the same rewards, regardless of their choices. A world of clones wearing their identical government-issued clothes.

It would be wonderful if reading this has convinced you that free-market capitalism is not the problem with the world but rather the solution. The free market and true capitalism are almost miraculous, because free-market capitalism can order an economy without direction. The spontaneous order generated by free markets is reminiscent of how the human body or any complex organism functions. Much like the government, the conscious mind is incapable of regulating the mechanisms that allow the organism to flourish. Instead, the cells in an organism, much like the citizens in a national economy, act in their best interest and do what they must to live, grow, and reproduce. The drive of producers and consumers to pursue their unique wants and desires by negotiating value with each other is what free markets do best. Free, uncorrupted capitalism is the only rational solution to humanity's problems.

> **The free market does not need managing. Every attempt to do so will make the world worse, not better.**

For those of you who started this book with socialist leanings, I applaud your imagining a better world; we all should. However, I hope you've learned enough in our time together to understand there's more to making a better world than dreams, and the evidence shows that free-market capitalism is the answer. Can we still make the world better? You bet! You can help by holding the government accountable for its failures. You can also join citizens' groups and protest crony capitalism. Encourage your elected representatives to help pass legislation to prevent those who would abuse the free market. But also encourage them to resist the temptation to allow the government to manage the economy, even slightly. The free market does not need managing. Every attempt to do so will make the world worse, not better. Free-market capitalism is the economics of hope—of investing today for a better future tomorrow.

When I began this book, I thought *Why Socialism Struggles* was a catchy title, and I stuck with it for that reason. It must have worked, since you picked up the book and (I hope) read it to the end. I would be remiss if I failed to point out that the conversational title belies the harm socialism has done to countless individuals and economies. While true, saying socialism struggles does not begin to convey the seriousness of the evil it has wrought. It doesn't merely struggle; it sucks. By now you understand the differences between democratic socialism and true socialism and realize that when a government assigns value for the people (socialism) instead of letting the people choose what is valuable to them (capitalism), their economy will not flourish for one simple reason: You cannot force excellence. In a free market economy like ours, citizens get to choose what they value, instead of being forced to like what the government tells them to value. We have had this freedom in the United States since 1776, and it is my sincere hope that we remain a free capitalist society—not only for our benefit but also for the benefit of generations to come.

Acknowledgments

They say no man is an island, and that's certainly true in my work on this book. I must thank my awesome publishing team, Dee Kerr, Benito Salazar, Rebecca Logan, Diana Ceres, Pam Nordberg, Diana Coe, Killian Piraro, Laurie MacQueen, Valerie Howard, and Chelsea Richards, who believed in this project and helped it become a reality. I also thank my son Ray and his wife, Carol, for their encouragement and all their hours of work on the initial editing. I thank my good friend Scott for his editing and support. Most of all, I thank my wonderful wife, Shay, for always being there to help. Throughout this process, she has been a teammate, a coach, and a cheerleader. I couldn't have done it without her.

Notes

INTRODUCTION

1. Frank Newport and Andrew Dugan, "Partisan Differences Growing on a Number of Issues," Gallup, August 3, 2017, https://news.gallup.com/opinion/polling-matters/215210/partisan-differences-growing-number-issues.aspx.

CHAPTER 1

1. Democratic Socialists of America, "What Is Democratic Socialism?," accessed November 22, 2024, https://www.dsausa.org/about-us/what-is-democratic-socialism/.

CHAPTER 2

1. Mary J. Ortner, "Captain Nathan Hale (1755–1776)," Connecticut Society of the Sons of the American Revolution, accessed December 18, 2024, https://www.sarconnecticut.org/captain-nathan-hale-1755-1776-2/.
2. Author's translation. The original text reads: "For this comunitie (so farr as it was) was found to breed much confusion & discontent, and retard much imploymēt that would have been to their benefite and comforte.

For ye yong-men that were most able and fitte for labour & service did repine that they should spend their time & streingth to worke for other mens wives and children, with out any recompence. The strong, or man of parts, had no more in devission of victails & cloaths, then he that was weake and not able to doe a quarter ye other could; this was thought injuestice. The aged and graver men to be ranked and [97] equalised in labours, and victails, cloaths, &c., with ye meaner & yonger sorte, thought it some indignite & disrespect unto them. And for mens wives to be commanded to doe servise for other men, as dresing their meate, washing their cloaths, &c., they deemd it a kind of slaverie, neither could many husbands well brooke it." William Bradford, *Of Plimoth Plantation* (Wright and Potter, 1898), 163, https://www.gutenberg.org/files/24950/24950-h/24950-h.htm.

CHAPTER 3

1. Callum Jones, "Asteroid Being Captured by NASA Worth $10,000,000,000,000,000,000,000 Would Make Everyone on Earth a Billionaire," UNILAD, April 18, 2024, https://www.unilad.com/technology/nasa/nasa-asteroid-16-psyche-earth-billionaire-028883-20240418.

2. David C. McClelland, *The Achieving Society* (Martino Fine, 2010).

CHAPTER 4

1. USGS, "How Much Gold Has Been Found in the World?," February 2, 2024, https://www.usgs.gov/faqs/how-much-gold-has-been-found-world.

2. US Department of Labor, "Union Members—2024," January 28, 2025, https://www.bls.gov/news.release/pdf/union2.pdf.

3. Lawrence Mishel and Jessica Scheider, "As Union Membership Has Fallen, the Top 10 Percent Have Been Getting a Larger Share of Income," Economic Policy Institute, May 24, 2016, https://www.epi.org/publication/as-union-membership-has-fallen-the-top-10-percent-have-been-getting-a-larger-share-of-income/.

CHAPTER 5

1. Chase Peterson-Withorn, ed., "The 400 Richest People in America," *Forbes*, accessed February 2, 2025, https://www.forbes.com/forbes-400/.

2. David C. McClelland, *The Achieving Society* (Martino Fine, 2010).

CHAPTER 6

1. US Census Bureau, *Census for 1820* (Gales and Seaton, 1821), https://www.census.gov/library/publications/1821/dec/1820a.html.

2. US Census Bureau, *Fourteenth Census of the United States Taken in the Year 1920*, vol. 1, *Population, 1920: Number and Distribution of Inhabitants* (Government Printing Office, 1921), https://www.census.gov/library/publications/1921/dec/vol-01-population.html.

3. Tyler Anbinder, *Plentiful Country: The Great Potato Famine and the Making of Irish New York* (Little, Brown, 2024).

4. US Census Bureau, *Census for 1820*; US Census Bureau, *Fourteenth Census of the United States Taken in the Year 1920*.

5. US Census Bureau, *The Statistics of the Population of the United States, June 1, 1970* (Government Printing Office, 1972), https://www.census.gov/library/publications/1872/dec/1870a.html; US Census Bureau, *Report on Population of the United States at the Eleventh Census: 1890* (Government Printing Office, 1895), https://www2.census.gov/library/publications/decennial/1890/volume-01/1890-population-part-1.pdf.

6. Eric Morris, "From Horse Power to Horsepower," *Access* 30, no. 10 (2007), https://escholarship.org/uc/item/6sm968t2.

7. Marie Concannon, "Prices and Wages by Decade: Intro," University of Missouri Libraries, June 13, 2025, https://libraryguides.missouri.edu/pricesandwages/home.

8. Federal Reserve Bank of St. Louis, "Gross Domestic Product per Capita," January 30, 2025, https://fred.stlouisfed.org/series/A939RC0Q052SBEA.

9. Statista, "Average Life Expectancy from Birth in the World and Selected Countries or Regions in Years Between 1820 and 2020," 2022, https://www.statista.com/statistics/1302736/global-life-expectancy-by-region-country-historical/.

10. Lam Thuy Vo, "Child Labor in America, 1920," NPR, August 17, 2012, https://www.npr.org/sections/money/2012/08/16/158925367/child-labor-in-america-1920.

11. Dave Roos, "The Origins of the Five-Day Work Week in America," History, August 26, 2024, https://www.history.com/news/five-day-work-week-labor-movement.

12. John Ransom, "State Teachers' Union Admits Marxist Platform Points from Assembly," *The Lion*, May 3, 2023, https://readlion.com/state-teachers-union-admits-marxist-platform-points-from-assembly/.

13. Melanie Asmar, "Denver Has the Largest Test Score Gaps by Race in the State," Chalkbeat Colorado, August 22, 2022, https://www.chalkbeat.org/colorado/2022/8/22/23313729/denver-test-score-gaps-largest-in-colorado-literacy-math-cmas/.

14. World Bank Group, "Gini Index," accessed February 2, 2025, https://data.worldbank.org/indicator/SI.POV.GINI.

15. US Bureau of Labor Statistics, "34.7 Percent of Business Establishments Born in 2013 Were Still Operating in 2023," *TED: The Economics Daily*, January 12, 2024, https://www.bls.gov/opub/ted/2024/34-7-percent-of-business-establishments-born-in-2013-were-still-operating-in-2023.htm.

16. R. J. Rummel, *Death by Government: Genocide and Mass Murder Since 1900* (Taylor and Francis, 1994).

17. Eileen Sullivan, "Growing Number of Chinese Migrants Are Crossing the Southern Border," *New York Times*, November 24, 2023, https://www.nytimes.com/2023/11/24/us/politics/china-migrants-us-border.html.

18. John Esten Cooke, *Virginia: A History of the People* (Houghton Mifflin, 1883), 109, https://archive.org/details/virginiahistoryo02cook/page/n11/mode/2up.

19. George Percy, "Jamestown, 1609–10: 'Starving Time,'" National Humanities Center, accessed December 19, 2024, https://nationalhumanitiescenter.org/pds/amerbegin/settlement/text2/JamestownPercyRelation.pdf.

20. Matthew Page Andrews, *Virginia: The Old Dominion* (Dietz Press, 1949), 61, https://archive.org/details/virginiaolddomin0000andr/page/60/mode/2up.

21. US Patent and Trademark Office, "Table of Issue Years and Patent Numbers, for Selected Document Types Issued Since 1836," February 3, 2025, https://www.uspto.gov/web/offices/ac/ido/oeip/taf/issuyear.htm.

22. J. Bradford De Long, "Estimates of World GDP, One Million B.C.–Present," 1998, https://delong.typepad.com/print/20061012_LRWGDP.pdf; International Monetary Fund, "GDP per Capita, Current Prices," 2025, https://www.imf.org/external/datamapper/NGDPDPC@WEO/OEMDC/ADVEC/WEOWORLD.

CHAPTER 7

1. George B. Moseley, "The U.S. Health Care Non-System, 1908–2008," *Virtual Mentor* 10, no. 5 (2008): 324–331.

2. Alex Tabarrok, "Physician and Nurse Incomes Have Increased Tremendously," *Marginal Revolution*, May 29, 2019, https://marginalrevolution.com/marginalrevolution/2019/05/physician-and-nurse-incomes-have-increased-tremendously.html.

3. Jonathan Tepper and Denise Hearn, *The Myth of Capitalism: Monopolies and the Death of Competition* (Wiley, 2019), 115.

4. Tepper and Hearn, *The Myth of Capitalism*, 305.

5. Tepper and Hearn, *The Myth of Capitalism*, xxii.

6. "Should Shareholders Be Personally Liable for the Torts of Their Corporations?," *Yale Law Journal* 76 (1967), https://doi.org/10.2307/794911.

7. Eric Wuestewald, "The Long, Expensive History of Defense Rip-Offs," *Mother Jones*, December 18, 2013, https://www.motherjones.com/politics/2013/12/defense-military-waste-cost-timeline/.

8. J. Justin Wilson, "Kentucky Governor Signs Bill Untangling Hair Braiders from Unnecessary Regulations," Institute for Justice, June 22, 2016, https://ij.org/press-release/kentucky-governor-signs-bill-untangling-hair-braiders-unnecessary-regulations/.

9. US Census Bureau, *Historical Statistics of the United States, 1789–1945* (US Government Printing Office, 1949), 200.

10. Sarah Pruitt, "How a Deadly Railroad Strike Led to the Labor Day Holiday," History, August 25, 2023, https://www.history.com/news/labor-day-pullman-railway-strike-origins.

11. Nina Teicholz, *The Big Fat Surprise: Why Butter, Meat and Cheese Belong in a Healthy Diet* (Simon and Schuster, 2014), 49.

12. Teicholz, *The Big Fat Surprise*, 59.

13. Rajiv Chowdhury, Samantha Warnakula, Setor Kunutsor, et al., "Association of Dietary, Circulating, and Supplement Fatty Acids with Coronary Risk: A Systematic Review and Meta-Analysis," *Annals of Internal Medicine* 160, no. 6 (2014), https://www.acpjournals.org/doi/10.7326/M13-1788?resultClick=3.

14. Agence France-Presse, "FDA Rewrites Rules of 'Healthy' Foods for First Time in 30 Years," *Science Alert*, December 20, 2024, https://www.sciencealert.com/fda-rewrites-rules-of-healthy-foods-for-first-time-in-30-years.

15. Maria Luz Fernandez and Ana Gabriela Murillo, "Is There a Correlation Between Dietary and Blood Cholesterol? Evidence from Epidemiological Data and Clinical Interventions," *Nutrients* 14, no. 10 (2022): 2168.

16. Luise Light, "A Fatally Flawed Food Guide," *Food Inc.*, 2004, http://www.whale.to/a/light.html.

17. Light, "A Fatally Flawed Food Guide."

18. Samuel D. Emmerich, Cheryl D. Fryar, Bryan Stierman, and Cynthia L. Ogden, "Obesity and Severe Obesity Prevalence in Adults: United States, August 2021–August 2023," *NCHS Data Brief*, no. 508 (2024), https://dx.doi.org/10.15620/cdc/159281.

19. Teicholz, *The Big Fat Surprise*, 49.

CHAPTER 8

1. Our World in Data, "Global GDP over the Long Run," May 16, 2024, https://ourworldindata.org/grapher/global-gdp-over-the-long-run?tab=table.

2. Our World in Data, "Global GDP."

3. Max Roser, "Extreme Poverty: How Far Have We Come, and How Far Do We Still Have to Go?," Our World in Data, August 27, 2023, https://ourworldindata.org/extreme-poverty-in-brief.

4. Federal Reserve Bank of St. Louis, "Poverty Status of Families by Type of Family: All Families with and Without Children Under 18 Years, Below Poverty Threshold," January 1, 2023, https://fred.stlouisfed.org/series/HSTPOVARWWCU18YAFBPP.

5. Erica York, "Summary of the Latest Federal Income Tax Data, 2023 Update," Tax Foundation, January 26, 2023, https://taxfoundation.org/data/all/federal/summary-latest-federal-income-tax-data-2023-update/.

6. "Cell Phone Statistics, 2024," *Consumer Affairs*, December 2, 2024, https://www.consumeraffairs.com/cell_phones/cell-phone-statistics.html.

7. Rakesh Kochhas, "The State of the American Middle Class: Who Is in It and Key Trends from 1970 to 2023," Pew Research Center, May 31, 2024, https://www.pewresearch.org/race-and-ethnicity/2024/05/31/the-state-of-the-american-middle-class/.

CHAPTER 9

1. Edward U. Lorenz, "Predictability: Does the Flap of a Butterfly's Wings in Brazil Set Off a Tornado in Texas?," paper presented at American Association for the Advancement of Science (AAAS) 139th meeting, December 29, 1972.

2. Douglas W. Cardell, "An Investigation into the Likelihood That a Centrally Planned Economy Can Provide Greater Economic Good than Spontaneous Order Created by the Free Market," doctoral diss., Liberty University, 2022, https://digitalcommons.liberty.edu/doctoral/3719/.

3. Ecclesiastes 11:1–3 (New International Version).

4. Cardell, "An Investigation."

5. Geoff Colvin, *Talent Is Overrated: What Really Separates World-Class Performers from Everybody Else* (Portfolio, 2010), 2.

6. Dan Bang and Chris D. Frith, "Making Better Decisions in Groups," *Royal Society Open Science* 4, no. 8 (2017), https://royalsocietypublishing.org/doi/pdf/10.1098/rsos.170193.

7. Philip E. Tetlock, *Expert Political Judgment: How Good Is It? How Can We Know?* (Princeton University Press, 2005), 39–40.

8. Michael S. McPherson and Morton Woen Schapiro, "US Higher Education Finance," in *Handbook of the Economics of Education*, vol. 2, ed. Eric Hanushek and Finis Welch (North-Holland, 2006): 1403–1434; Camilo Maldonado, "Price of College Increasing Almost 8 Times Faster than Wages," *Forbes*, July 24, 2018, https://www.forbes.com/sites/camilomaldonado/2018/07/24/price-of-college-increasing-almost-8-times-faster-than-wages/#bcb1c5166c1d.

9. National Center for Education Statistics, "Average Undergraduate Tuition, Fees, Room, and Board Rates Charged for Full-Time Students in Degree-Granting Postsecondary Institutions, by Level and Control of Institution: Selected Academic Years, 1963–64 through 2022–23," accessed December 30, 2024, https://nces.ed.gov/programs/digest/d23/tables/dt23_330.10.asp.

10. Xiaomeng Liu, Hongyan Gao, Lu Sun, and Jun Yao, "Generic Air-Gen Effect in Nanoporous Materials for Sustainable Energy Harvesting from Air Humidity," *Advanced Materials* 36, no. 12 (2024), https://doi.org/10.1002/adma.202300748.

About the Author

DOUG CARDELL is a seventh-generation American patriot. His fourth great-grandfather and several other relatives died fighting in the American Revolution. Doug is a veteran of the US Air Force Reserve and the New Mexico National Guard. As such, Doug swore to support and defend the United States like each of the six generations before him. That oath had no expiration date. He believes the biggest threat to the country today is an increasing view that socialism is a viable answer to our problems, and this book is his defense against that threat.

Doug is an economist and economic policy expert. He has served as an aide to a member of Congress, a corporate CEO, and a professor of mathematics. He holds advanced degrees and certificates from the University of Arizona, the Massachusetts Institute of Technology, and the University of Phoenix, as well as a PhD in economic policy from Liberty University. His expertise in economics, from both a theoretical and a practical standpoint, coupled with his expertise in mathematics and modeling, as well as high success as an educator, makes him uniquely qualified to explain economics and evaluate economic systems and ideas.